Devoted to Christ

Devoted to Christ

*Missiological Reflections
in Honor of Sherwood G. Lingenfelter*

Edited by Christopher L. Flanders
Foreword by C. Douglas McConnell

☙PICKWICK *Publications* · Eugene, Oregon

DEVOTED TO CHRIST
Missiological Reflections in Honor of Sherwood G. Lingenfelter

Copyright © 2019 Wipf and Stock. All rights reserved. Except for brief quotations in critical publications or reviews, no part of this book may be reproduced in any manner without prior written permission from the publisher. Write: Permissions, Wipf and Stock Publishers, 199 W. 8th Ave., Suite 3, Eugene, OR 97401.

Pickwick Publications
An Imprint of Wipf and Stock Publishers
199 W. 8th Ave., Suite 3
Eugene, OR 97401

www.wipfandstock.com

PAPERBACK ISBN: 978-1-5326-1183-4
HARDCOVER ISBN: 978-1-5326-1185-8
EBOOK ISBN: 978-1-5326-1184-1

Cataloguing-in-Publication data:

Names: Flanders, Christopher L., editor. | McConnell, C. Douglas, foreword.

Title: Devoted to Christ : missiological reflections in honor of Sherwood G. Lingenfelter. / edited by Christopher L. Flanders; foreword by C. Douglas McConnell.

Description: Eugene, OR: Pickwick Publications, 2019 | Includes bibliographical references.

Identifiers: ISBN 978-1-5326-1183-4 (paperback) | ISBN 978-1-5326-1185-8 (hardcover) | ISBN 978-1-5326-1184-1 (ebook)

Subjects: LCSH: Lingenfelter, Sherwood G. | Missions—Anthropological aspects. | Intercultural communication—Religious aspects—Christianity.

Classification: BV2061 D48 2019 (print) | BV2061 (ebook)

Manufactured in the USA.   SEPTEMBER 17, 2019

Dedicated to Sherwood Lingenfelter. Teacher, mentor, friend.

Contents

Contributors / ix
Foreword by C. Douglas McConnell / xi
Introduction / xiii

1. Anthropology, Missiology, and the Witch / 1
   Robert J. Priest

2. Navigating The Cross-Cultural Dynamics of Global Mission Organizations / 16
   Donna R. Downes

3. The State of Minority Languages in the Twenty-First Century / 30
   John R. Watters

4. Independence to Interdependence / 50
   Paul R. Gupta

5. Navigating Power / 65
   Anita Koeshall

6. Generosity and Reciprocity in Thai Society / 79
   Larry S. Persons

7. Activating Kingdom Agents / 92
   Alan Weaver

8. Leadership and Patron-Client Structures in Thailand / 106
   Lorraine Dierck

9. The Essence of Leadership: Mission From a Position of Weakness / 119
   Paul Yonggap Jeong

10 Practical and Missiological Implications for the Transformation of Machismo / 130
   Wilmer Villacorta

11 There is No Such Thing as "Honor" or "Honor Cultures" / 145
   Christopher L. Flanders

Bibliography / 167

Contributors

Dr. Lorraine Dierck—Field Leader, World Outreach International, Bangkok, Thailand

Dr. Donna R. Downes—Associate Professor of Global Leadership, Fuller Theological Seminary, Pasadena, California

Dr. Christopher L. Flanders—Associate Professor of Missions, Abilene Christian University, Abilene, Texas

Dr. Paul R. Gupta—President and Director of Hindustan Bible Institute, Chennai, India

Dr. Paul Yonggap Jeong—International Director of Vision for the Kingdom and Adjunct Professor of Intercultural Studies, Fuller Theological Seminary, Pasadena, California

Dr. Anita Koeshall—Associate Professor of Intercultural Studies, Assemblies of God Theological Seminary, Springfield, Missouri

Dr. C. Douglas McConnell—Provost Emeritus and Professor of Leadership & Intercultural Studies, Fuller Theological Seminary, Pasadena, California

Dr. Larry S. Persons—CEO, CQ Leadership Consulting and Adjunct Professor of Leadership, Sasin Graduate Institute of Business Administration, Chulalongkorn University, Bangkok, Thailand

Contributors

Dr. Robert J. Priest—Professor of Anthropology, Taylor University, Upland, Indiana

Dr. Wilmer Villacorta—Assistant Professor of Intercultural Studies, Fuller Theological Seminary, Pasadena, California

Dr. John R. Watters—Former President and current Special Advisor to the Executive Director, SIL International, Dallas, Texas

Dr. Alan Weaver—Vice President of Expansion and Curriculum, Entrust, Colorado Springs, Colorado and Affiliate Professor of Leadership, Fuller Theological Seminary, Pasadena, California

Foreword

C. Douglas McConnell

Last week the faculty of the School of Intercultural Studies voted on the student awards for 2018–2019. In the twenty years since Sherwood Lingenfelter joined our faculty, he consistently nominates his mentorees and importantly, in the eyes of the faculty, they always deserve the honor. Anyone who knows Sherwood is not surprised by this addition to his legacy of honoring others. It is not an obsession; it is a gift.

Sherwood Lingenfelter is an anthropologist in the field of missiological studies. In the tradition of the Fuller anthropologists—Alan Tippett, Charles Kraft, Paul Hiebert, Daniel Shaw—Sherwood integrates the insights of anthropological scholarship with practical theology in service of mission studies. His works each contribute to our mission practice in ways that impact the global missionary movement. From insights into ministering cross-culturally to leading cross-culturally, Sherwood brings the best of anthropology to the best in missiology. Beyond his scholarship in publications and service in institutional leadership, Sherwood served as an outstanding educator through the regional accrediting association, Western Association of Schools and Colleges, completing his service in the position of Chair of the Board of Commissioners.

My first meeting with Sherwood was traveling to the faculty retreat in 1999, the year we both joined the faculty. Sherwood was the new dean of the School of World Mission, coming from Biola University where he served as provost. I knew of Sherwood through his writings, so on this first meeting, I was excited both to get to know my new boss and to engage his scholarship as an anthropologist. My respect for his scholarship quickly grew into admiration of his mature leadership embodied in his attentive communication. True to his reputation, he was humble, honest, and kind, qualities intrinsic to honor.

We became close personal colleagues in the years ahead. Before moving to Pasadena, I was invited to stay in the Lingenfelter's home while I was teaching on campus. All who know Sherwood are aware that his favorite place is beside Judy, his beloved wife, and colleague, who together freely share their lives and home with others. Hospitality is yet another personal quality.

Two unique transitions further characterize my relationship to Sherwood Lingenfelter. When Sherwood became provost of Fuller Theological Seminary in 2002, I was appointed his successor as dean of the school. In 2011 when Sherwood retired as provost, I was again appointed his successor as provost of the seminary. In each of these leadership transitions, Sherwood exhibited the same qualities adding a special blend of empowerment and support. His public acknowledgment of my appointment was always combined with a firm statement of his confidence in my ability. Privately, he reinforced that confidence by affirming and advising my various assessments of the institution in our conversations. His advice waited for times when I requested or needed it. His actions were empowering in every instance.

As I reflect on the past twenty years of service beside Sherwood Lingenfelter, I am struck by the simple fact that he is and has always been a dedicated follower of Christ. His relationship with his family demonstrates the value of love and commitment. With his colleagues, he is a disciple who can live authentically; humble in success and contrite in disappointments. In mentoring, he is kind, considerate, and critical, instilling a sense of accomplishment that stirs each one to be the best they can be. He is a remarkable friend and a follower of Christ, who like the Apostle, could appropriately say, "Follow my example, as I follow the example of Christ" (1 Cor 11:1, NIV).

In these pages that follow, the authors provide ample evidence of their commitment to the qualities of our friend Sherwood Lingenfelter. Together we honor him in the genre of scholarship that he has so ably upheld throughout his career. It is also with special thanks that I want to acknowledge the tireless efforts of Professor Chris Flanders, the editor of this volume. He is genuinely one of the exemplars of the Lingenfelter tradition.

C. DOUGLAS MCCONNELL, PHD
Provost Emeritus and Professor of Leadership & Intercultural Studies
Fuller Theological Seminary

Introduction

CHRISTOPHER L. FLANDERS

Several years ago, when Sherwood made public his plan to retire from full-time teaching and administrative work, I knew it was time to begin work on a volume that would draw together colleagues and former students that represented his broad and deep impact. In other words, it was the opportunity to produce a festschrift.

The German term "festschrift" literally means "festival writing." In a sense, by assembling these essays together, we are throwing a party to celebrate the impact of the life and work of Sherwood. But, a festschrift is also an exercise in social honor. That is, all festschriften aim at the public recognition of an honoree. It is entirely appropriate that I have the distinct honor of editing the essays these authors have produced to honor Sherwood. This is because my relationship with Sherwood Lingenfelter has been an extended exercise in social honor.

I first met Sherwood at a seminar in Chiang Mai Thailand. I asked him to lunch, to which he agreed. At the beginning of the lunch, I immediately informed him that I had already determined to pursue a PhD at a school other than Fuller Theological Seminary, the one at which he was currently teaching. Unfazed, he noted how excellent the other school was and then proceeded to honor me with insight, encouragement, and helpful advice for pursuing doctoral work in anthropology and intercultural studies. I later changed my direction, applied to and was accepted at Fuller, and did work in the area of social honor and facework theory. I was blessed to spend 3 years as Sherwood's teaching assistant. The numerous lessons I learned from him I can summarize in these words: humility, excellence, and honor.

In particular, I noted how a distinguished scholar and administrator at a world-class seminary routinely demonstrated to students and colleagues the greatest levels of honoring others above himself. As I waded deeper into anthropological and social-psychological studies, it struck me how I could see in tangible fashion through Sherwood's life the very lessons I was learning about social honor. He was always learning from those around him. He, the honorable teacher, dean, and provost, opened himself up to being taught by others. He did this with incredible humility, admitting to his own faults and cultural blinders. He made it a habit to heap honor on others by giving credit, opportunity, and attention.

One example stands out. In his installation ceremony as provost, I was profoundly moved by how he manifested what my studies were teaching me about the dynamics of social honor. In an extraordinary example of diffused social honor, Sherwood, in his speech, drew attention not to himself or his credentials, but to the entire community it took to make an educational institution run well. Instead of claiming the appropriate social honor of becoming provost, Sherwood shared it. He accepted the *proper reward for virtue* (Aristotle's definition of "honor") and then simply passed it on to others. Clearly following the example of Christ as Paul notes in the book of Philippians, Sherwood did not consider becoming provost (or dean, or professor) something to be held on to or exploited for personal gain. Rather, he emptied himself of the honor that he had legitimately achieved and was being ascribed, which was in fact a major purpose of that installation ceremony of distinction. In this way, he showed himself to be not only one who was *honored* but also one who was *honorable*.

Ideally, a festschrift is not simply a retrospective look back, but also an exercise in prospective anticipation. That is, by highlighting distinguished work by a scholar a festschrift calls readers to imitate the virtues of the honoree. Indeed, this is one of the most powerful dynamics of social honor. Acts of honorification, such as the production of a festschrift, create a type of social gravity that draws others toward what is displayed as worthy of honor.

This dedicated volume is a tribute that calls Christian anthropologists to remain centered on the mission of God in Christ. And, it is a call to missiologists and missionaries to apply to the mission of God rigorous, critical, and current anthropological theory. Sherwood's published books have enjoyed extraordinary success, primarily due to the ways he demonstrates how anthropological theory is useful in exegeting cultures and leadership. Indeed, *Ministering Cross-Culturally* is now published in a third edition with more than 125,000 copies in print. This is an extraordinarily high number for a mission text. The power of his life, however, is also due to his unwavering devotion to Christ and to living a life of obedient excellence. This is the legacy of Sherwood Lingenfelter. This is the legacy that we are delighted to honor and imitate.

Paul tells believers in Romans 13:7 they are obligated to render what is owed to different parties. In particular, Paul commands the Roman Christians to pay off the debt of respect and honor to those whom it is owed. It is our duty, an obligation of honor. All who know Sherwood would agree that the global Christian community owes a profound debt for his devotion, example, and work. This volume is but a small token paid toward the enormous debt we owe him.

CHRISTOPHER L. FLANDERS
Associate Professor of Missions at Abilene Christian University

1

Anthropology, Missiology, and the Witch

ROBERT J. PRIEST

While cultures vary enormously, one surprisingly recurrent pattern involves people attributing affliction and death to malevolent third parties. That is, people accuse their neighbors or family members of harming and murdering others through occult power. While cultures historically varied widely in whether this power was described as psychic, magical, or mediated through sentient spirits, the core idea that misfortune and death are to be blamed on evil human beings is surprisingly widespread. Anthropologists typically translate indigenous terms for such a person as "witch" or "sorcerer/sorceress."

Clarity in what we mean by a word is important. The word football, for example, can confusingly refer to either of two very different games. And, while a modern Wiccan may apply the term "witch" to herself, this is another game, as it were, from what anthropologists and missionaries have encountered across a wide variety of cultures and which anthropologists treat under the term witch. While America has many Wiccans or Neo-Pagans who would self-identify as "witch," such does not fall under the traditional rubric of "witch" that involves malevolence or harm directed at others. In a recent survey of 48 American seminarians, only 4 percent said they had ever known a colleague, relative, or neighbor to be accused by anyone of harming someone through witchcraft, with one respondent (2 percent) clarifying in a note that he or she only experienced this while living overseas. In contrast, in a survey of 161 African seminarians, 85 percent reported that one or more of their colleagues, relatives, or neighbors had been accused of harming others through witchcraft. It is the latter meaning I address in this paper. As historically used by anthropologists, the term "witch" applies to *a male or female human being who is said to be the cause of another's misfortune, sickness, and/or death by means of psychic or other occult power*. In ethnographic writings this is also the meaning of sorcerer/sorceress, although sorcery generally also implies that the harm is caused through learned and acquired, self-consciously exercised powers, which is not necessarily true of the witch idea.

While anthropologists encounter a wide variety of indigenous terms for healers, mediums, priests, diviners, magicians, shamans, witch categories differ from these in one important respect. Shamans, healers, priests, magicians, diviners, mediums, and pastors all have a social existence that is relatively straightforward. Their identity is agreed on. One can interview them about their identity and role, and under the right circumstances watch them at work. But indigenous categories, which anthropologists translate as witch, reference an identity constructed through discourse but whose actual social existence is problematic. That is, indigenous labels which anthropologists translate as "witch" exist primarily in discourse, more specifically in gossip and accusation, with the persons that others accuse of being witches usually, though not always, denying the attribution.

The label here is a contested one. Indeed in many cultures it is thought that witches might not be aware that they themselves are witches. Thus, self-knowledge is irrelevant to whether others construct one as a witch. While sometimes people "confess" that they have harmed or killed someone else through witchcraft, this is typically under psycho-social dynamics that lead anthropologists and historians to distrust the confessions as reliable. To take a simple example, in Salem, Massachusetts the only people killed as witches were those accused of being witches who refused to agree with the accusation.[1] The accused that did "confess" were not killed. Such motivated confession is hardly a reliable confirmation that such persons really are causing harm to others through witchcraft. Someone who "confesses" that at night they secretly traveled thousands of miles on a "witch airplane" to kill a distant relative is hardly the sort of claim that can be confirmed. Therefore, the witch category appears to exist primarily through discourses

---

1. Hill, *Delusion of Satan*; Hoffer, *Salem Witchcraft*.

about witches, especially gossip and accusation, motivated claims-making discourses which, under analysis, appear to be created and sustained through psycho-social processes rightly distrusted by scholars.

Anthropologists have attempted to explain the pervasive presence of witch discourses in a variety of ways. First, they have stressed people's need for cognitive explanations. People who face affliction, illness, and death need ways to make sense of and to explain their affliction.[2] Some cultures make sense of affliction and death through what Richard Shweder[3] calls moral causal ontologies where, like Job's four friends, wise counselors of the culture unite in generating narratives intended to validate the truth that the sufferer's own moral failures caused his or her own suffering. Wise counselors in other cultures (diviners, healers, shamans) make sense of affliction and death through interpersonal causal ontologies[4] by identifying a human third party felt to have less than exemplary feelings for the afflicted and who can be blamed for causing the affliction. Again a whole community expends great effort in discursively constructing the truth of the witch who is to be blamed for the affliction. In either case, the afflicted now have a way to interpret and understand their affliction. On this understanding, people are more satisfied with a cognitive explanation of their affliction than with no explanation at all.

Other anthropologists point out that witch discourses are really discourses about human evil, about selfishness, lust, greed, gluttony, envy, resentment, and animosity. Since people who exemplify such asocial or sinful tendencies are the ones most likely to be accused of being a witch, that is, accused of being the cause of another's affliction or death, and since those identified as witches are often horribly mistreated, there is high motivation for people to avoid such asocial tendencies. On this understanding, witch discourses function to buttress moral virtues by motivating people to avoid the immoral attributes likely to result in them being accused of being witches. Other anthropologists adopt a hydraulic pressure-release model of society, theorizing that periodic unleashing of violence against supposed witches helps to siphon off and resolve social stress and aggression, returning society to a state of equilibrium.

While historians of Europe emphasized the horrific consequences of witch discourses and accompanying actions, many anthropologists

---

2. Evans-Pritchard, *Witchcraft, Oracles, and Magic*.
3. Shweder, *Why Do Men Barbecue?*
4. Shweder, *Why Do Men Barbecue?*

adopted functionalist analyses, searching for positive explanations of witch discourses and downplaying the negative consequences for the accused. However, when anthropologists provide descriptive detail, it is clear that being labeled a witch is often consequential. Clyde Kluckhohn,[5] for example, interpreted Navaho witch accusations as functioning to displace aggression and bring social equilibrium. But embedded in his ethnographic description was a more disturbing dimension. In the community of 500 people studied by Kluckhohn, 19 were accused of being witches, with another 10 already killed as witches. That is, in his data one out of every 20 to 25 people was accused of being a witch—many by their sons-in-law. The accused witch was often "tied down and not allowed to eat, drink or relieve himself until he confesses,"[6] with hot coals applied to the feet to encourage confession. Kluckhohn tells us that the violent killing of witches (with axes, clubs, guns) was common and that "the killing of witches is uniformly described as violently sadistic."[7] Whatever one thinks of the supposed positive functions of this for society, the negative consequences for real people are significant.

Furthermore, ethnography demonstrates that human relationships in witch-accusing societies are fraught with interpersonal hostilities, envy, and resentment. This means that whenever someone gets sick and faces death, they are often surrounded by many sinful people who plausibly can be understood as having desired their harm. That is, they are surrounded by people who in the moral logic of the culture ought to love the afflicted but who in fact exemplify the very sinful attributes (selfishness, envy, gluttony, greed, resentment, enmity, lack of love), which are said to motivate witches. In German we might say there are many who feel *schadenfreude*, a witch-like surge of joy at another's misfortune. Thus in cultures which attribute blame for each misfortune, there is high motivation on the part of many possible suspects to deflect attention off of themselves as possible witch and onto others. A whole community of sinners nervously denies their own sinful witchlike sentiments, and search for a consensus on some other socially marginal and vulnerable person that they can scapegoat as the witch. They attribute to this person the very sentiments they themselves exemplify, and join in acts of social exclusion or violence intended to remove evil from their midst. No one defends the accused, lest they themselves be accused.

5. Kluckhohn, *Navaho Witchcraft*.
6. Kluckhohn, *Navaho Witchcraft*, 48.
7. Kluckhohn, *Navaho Witchcraft*, 98.

Priest—Anthropology, Missiology, and the Witch

Another pattern that historians and anthropologists have widely observed is that accusations follow lines of hostility and resentment. A poor old widow, with no one to care for her, constantly asks neighbors and relatives for help or food. Neighbors and relatives often turn her away, but feel guilty when they do so, with their unacknowledged guilt transformed into resentment and hostility towards her as well as fear of her. People often fear and hate those they have sinned against (see Prov 28:1). The next time some affliction occurs, their guilt, resentment and hostility towards her is easily channeled into accusations that she is really a witch who has caused their affliction, someone who does not deserve help, and who in fact merits the resentment, hostility, and violence expressed towards her by her accusers. Alternatively, a man dies and his brothers unite in accusing his widow of killing him through witchery, justifying through the accusation their expropriation of marital assets. Again and again, when scholars have carefully tracked the direction of accusations they often find self-interested accusations, which reflect hostility, guilt, and hatred on the part of accusers towards the accused. In short, the very act of accusing someone of being a witch can itself become a harmful, malicious and self-interested act, with the accusers themselves sinning in the very act of accusing. According to historian and social critic René Girard,[8] it is less the individual being accused, than the whole community of self-righteous accusers, who most exemplify the attributes of Satan, the great accuser.

In most cultures that stress interpersonal causal ontologies there are religious healers, diviners, shamans, or witchdoctors whose professional authority is pivotal to the validation of such ontologies. Their medical diagnoses affirm that another person is to blame for the affliction. They construct their own power and authority on their supposed ability to combat the dangerous power of purported witches. As the anthropologist Michael Brown[9] has pointed out in an already classic article, while such healers are ostensibly in the business of healing, it is the very diagnostic system that they ratify and propagate that sows suspicion and retaliatory violence. The incredibly high rate of violence which Brown documents in Aguaruna society is grounded in witch ontologies fostered by shamans. Thus he argues that there is a dark side to religious healers who operate with interpersonal causal ontologies. They claim to bring life, but foster dynamics leading to death. Presumably he would also argue that there was a dark side to Cotton

---

8. Girard, *Violence and the Sacred*; *Scapegoat*; *Things Hidden*; *I See Satan fall*.
9. Brown, *Natural History*, 8–11.

Mather's endorsement of the witch ontologies underpinning violence in Salem.

When a community accuses a specific member to be the cause of community misfortunes, illness, and death, such is enormously consequential to the accused, who is now treated as outside of the community to whom moral obligation is due. The atrocities perpetrated on persons said to be witches have been and continues to be horrendous. And since envious resentment is thought to motivate witch evil, those most naturally suspected of envious resentment are those who are most needy and vulnerable, such as elderly widows or orphans. It is the weakest and most vulnerable members of society who most suffer the adverse consequences of a diagnostic system attributing misfortune and death to human third parties imagined as acting through evil occult means.

A quick example from the missiologist Neville Bartle[10] illustrates the realities here. In a largely Christian New Guinea village, split evenly between Anglicans and Nazarenes, a dispute left a marginal old widow feeling wronged, but without social recourse. Weeks later the wife of the village headman died, and the old woman was blamed for the death, accused of being a witch. She denied the charge, but was beaten until her ribs were cracked and her arm and hand bones were crushed, and so she eventually "confessed" that she was a witch and had two accomplices whom she named. She confessed to doing what witches are thought to do in her culture, stare at people till they became unconscious, and then operate, remove and eat the organs, and seal up the incision through occult powers. The victim would wake up not aware of what had happened and die a few days later. The two women she named confessed more quickly than she had, and thus were not beaten as severely. Neville Bartle, who arrived days later in the village with his missionary team describes the old woman as "the most pathetic, shriveled up woman I have ever seen." Locked up, she had not been given food or drink for 5 days. She had a high fever, and pus drained from her hand into a puddle in the ashes. A missionary gave her water and the Nazarene village pastor questioned the three women before the missionaries, where they reaffirmed their witch confessions. The old woman was then told, "Although she had committed many evil deeds, there was forgiveness and salvation through faith in Christ." The pastor "led the women in a sentence-by-sentence prayer of confession and repentance." The old woman died the next day.

---

10. Bartle, *Developing a Contextual Theology*; *Death, Witchcraft*.

Priest—Anthropology, Missiology, and the Witch

Anthropologists and missionaries often thought of "witchcraft accusations" as part of a primitive past, on its way out. But increasingly anthropologists are recognizing that modernity in many settings seems to actually stimulate higher levels of witchcraft anxieties and concerns.[11] Across New Guinea, Africa, the Caribbean, and parts of Asia and Latin America witch accusations are flourishing and taking new forms, one of the most startling being the exploding trend across many African countries (Nigeria, Congo, Angola or the Central African Republic) for young children to be blamed for the deaths of relatives, branded as witches.[12]

Recently, as I traveled in Africa on other business, I heard the following accounts: A Christian High Court Judge mentioned to me that in the last 30 days she had dealt with ten murder trials where young adults killed their fathers or grandfathers because a diviner had told them that these old men were really witches who were the cause of their misfortune. A seminary professor noted that among the Sukuma, where he worked, it was old women who were accused. According to research carried out by his students, police records in Mwanza, Tanzania from 2006-2010 show 473 lynchings of elderly widows accused of being witches. The director of a large orphanage told me that 30 percent of children being brought to his orphanage were rescued from being branded as witches supposedly to blame for the deaths of relatives. He told stories of atrocities perpetrated on these small children, sometimes by pastors—who in many cases have replaced the traditional diviners as the witch finders and cleansers. A seminary professor told me how others had accused him of being a witch, and I learned of other pastors who had to leave their pastorate when rumors that they were really witches achieved wide acceptance. Clearly there are a wide variety of pastoral issues involved in such witch accusations.

In my survey of 161 seminary students and faculty at a leading evangelical seminary in Africa (administered January 16, 2012), 85 percent report that at least one of their colleagues, relatives, or neighbors has been accused of harming others through witchcraft. Fully 34 percent of these report that the consequences for their relative or neighbor who was accused involved being killed, with 47 percent reporting the accused had property

---

11. Geschiere, *Modernity of Witchcraft*; Ashforth, *Witchcraft, Violence, and Democracy*; Priest, *Witches*, 30–32.

12. Aguilar Molina, *Invention of Child Witches*; Biehl, *Vita*; Boeck and Plissart, *Kinshasa*; Foxcroft, *Supporting Victims of Witchcraft Abuse*; Geschiere, *Modernity of Witchcraft*; Human Rights Watch, *What Future?*; La Fontaine, *Devil's Children*; Pereira, *Families, Churches, the State*; Ranger, *Scotland Yard*, 272–83.

destroyed or taken, 47 percent reporting that the accused was driven from their home or community, 52 percent saying the accused was beaten or physically attacked, and 84 percent reporting that the accused was shunned and avoided. Since the accused are often the elderly, widows, or orphans with no means of livelihood other than the charity and good graces of neighbors and relatives, being shunned or avoided has serious implications for life. Finally, two-thirds of seminary respondents reported that they suspected one or more of the people they knew who had been accused were in fact innocent of the charges.

Christian missionaries, local pastors, and theological leaders in societies stressing interpersonal causal ontologies face difficult challenges in assessing and responding to such witch discourses and retaliatory practices. There are many reasons for this. First, while t filled with stories of infertility, affliction, and death (the very subject matter which in many cultures triggers witch discourses) the Bible makes no reference to interpersonal causal ontologies purporting to explain misfortune. Had the book of Job been written in a Sukuma or Aguaruna cultural context, the four wise counselors would have unitedly focused their efforts on identifying a less-fortunate neighbor of Job, someone believed to envy his wealth or family, or who had expressed resentment or a grudge against him, and would have single-mindedly pursued consensus on this third human party to be blamed. But the Bible was not produced in a cultural context discursively saturated with an interpersonal-causal-ontology logic. Instead, numerous biblical texts involve dialog with moral causal ontologies of the culture—where cultural assumptions blamed the afflicted for their own suffering. *Nowhere in Scripture do we find anyone attributing affliction or death to a human third party acting through evil occult means.* To anyone who has lived with the witch-saturated discourses of the Aguaruna for example, as I have, where every death is blamed on a human witch, this total absence in Scripture of the very idea that misfortune is caused by human parties acting through evil occult means is startling. Of course this means that when missionaries encounter interpersonal causal ontologies in Peru, New Guinea, Angola, or Tanzania, they do not find any biblical teaching directly addressing the topic. This is a serious handicap. When missionaries encounter moral causal ontologies, they find rich biblical passages helping them provide assessment and correctives. But when they encounter interpersonal causal ontologies, they find no biblical passages that directly address such a cultural logic.

Priest—Anthropology, Missiology, and the Witch

Bible translation contributes to the challenge at multiple levels. In societies around the world, a range of indigenous terms exists for people thought to have unusual powers and knowledge. One set of terms entails the idea that certain people are at core evil, secretly bringing harm and death to others. Anthropologists historically translated these terms into English as "witch" or "sorcerer/sorceress." A second set of terms reference magico-religious professionals with unusual powers and/or knowledge typically thought to be exercised on behalf of others. These have been variously translated into English as shaman, magician, witchdoctor, traditional healer, diviner, or medium. While persons so categorized are sometimes said to also have the power to harm others, this is not generally the core meaning of these categories, and applying any of these categories to a person does not in itself entail any necessary idea that this person harms others. Anthropologists would *not* normally translate these terms into English as "witch" or "sorcerer."

With this as a backdrop, it is worth considering how Bible translations often seemingly affirm occult-killer (witch) beliefs. For example, in Matthew 2, the word *magi* (the plural of *magus*), rather than being translated with an indigenous term, is sometimes simply transliterated from Greek into other languages (as with Malagasy or Swahili or some English translations); or it may be translated as "wise or educated persons" (as in Mandarin, Kimeru, Moore, Twi, Yoruba, Kalenjin, Kikamba), or as those "knowledgeable about the stars" (Nuer, Sango, other versions of Mandarin and Swahili). But few translations follow the Greek in using the same term in Acts 8 and Acts 13 that is used in Matthew 2 (Bambara being an exception). Some translations of Acts 8 and 13 use indigenous terms for magico-religious professionals having unusual powers and claims to special knowledge (Nuer, Aguaruna, Amharic, Cambodian), but other translations use terms for Simon and/or Elymas which identifies them as occult killers—that is, which, following anthropological convention, we gloss in English as "witch/sorcerer" (Kimeru, Yoruba, Malagasy, Kikamba, Kalenjin). Needless to say none of these translations use this same witch/sorcery term for the *magi* of Matthew 2. Many Christians in societies that attribute misfortune and death to evil humans acting through occult power rely on Bible translations in their own languages which affirm that Simon and Elymas were exactly such occult killers. But these are not accurate translations. Simon, for example, had a public identity as wonder worker.[13] What he wished to purchase from

---

13. Not unlike those studied in Siegel, *Net of Magic*.

Peter was not the power to harm others (as a witch/sorcerer might), but the ability to publically impress and amaze others with his power. Again, when translations imply the woman at Endor (1 Sam 28) was an occult killer, rather than a medium, this too is mistranslation.

Perhaps the most important biblical text in this regard is Exodus 22:18 where the Israelites are not to allow *kashaph* to live. The exact meaning of *kashaph* is contested. In Exodus 7:11, the *kashaph* are part of Pharaoh's retinue of magico-religious professionals asked to perform power displays, and in Daniel 2:2, Nebuchadnezzar's cadre of *kashaph* are asked to divine his dream. In these two examples it appears that *kashaph* are magico-religious professionals who, among other things, divine dreams and perform power displays. The LXX translated *kashaph* as *pharmakous*, a translation consistent with the idea that these were magico-religious professionals of some sort. But when the Latin Vulgate translated *kashaph* as *maleficos*, this moved things more towards the witch/sorcery idea, a translation with consequences for European history.

While some translations of the Bible render *kashaph* with indigenous terms for professional magico-religious practitioners (such as in Korean or Cambodian Bibles) with no necessary implication of occult harm or murder, numerous Bible translations across Africa translate rather with terms meaning occult-killer (Kimeru, Lingala, Kalenjin, Yoruba, Malagasy, Twi, Swahili, Amharic, Bambara, Kikamba, Bobo, Dholuo). That is, where Kamba Christians read a Bible endorsing the traditional Kamba assumption that human third parties are to blame for misfortunes and death, third parties who are really serial murderers and who should thus be killed, Korean Christians find rather the shaman condemned, a figure in Korea not associated with killing others, but whom a jealous God insists must not be part of the people of God. Korean or Cambodian Christians read a different Bible at this point than most African Christians, or even than many English speakers. The Exodus 7:11 and Daniel 2:2 accounts would seem to better fit the Korean translation (where kings historically did avail themselves of shamans doing exactly the sort of things being asked for here), than the occult killer idea of many African translations. Some African translations consistently translate *kashaph* in all three passages (Exod 22:18, Exod 7:11, Dan 2:2) using the same indigenous term for evil occult-killer (Swahili, Yoruba, Malagasy, Amharic, Kikamba), although speakers of these languages concede that traditionally no one would ever call on such witches/sorcerers to interpret a dream, or would expect a king to have a public cadre of witches/sorcerers at his beck and call for public power displays. Perhaps because of this lack of fit, many African translations retain the witch/sorcery idea for the Exodus 22:18 passage calling for the death of the *kashaph*, but use other indigenous terms for public magico-religious professionals to translate *kashaph* in Exodus 7:11 and/or Daniel 2:2 (as in Kimeru, Lingala, Kalenjin, Twi, Bambara, Dholuo, Bobo). Repeatedly I have heard many African Christians (but by no means all) affirm that the Bible teaches the existence of humans who kill through witchcraft. And, it was Exodus 22:18 which they invariably pointed to as proof.

Missionaries historically were not only handicapped by biblical silence on the subject of interpersonal causal ontologies, and by a revered history of mistranslations, which seemingly ratified such ontologies, but they have also encountered translational challenges they failed to understand. When they entered societies featuring interpersonal causal ontologies, it was the figure of the witch that in these societies played the central role in cultural imaginings of evil. Rather than imagining ultimate evil as located in a supernatural being absolutely opposed to God and the good, such societies imagined ultimate evil as exemplified in human relatives or neighbors identified as witches. Part of what this meant was that the vocabulary of evil available for translation was a vocabulary inflected with witch associations, which meant that its very usage implied the reality of human witches.[14] Missionaries were decoded as proclaiming a message about witches. Among the Adioukrou of Côte d'Ivoire, for example, the Christian concept of "the devil" was translated for local Christians by *agn*, the indigenous word for witchcraft.[15] Or again, anthropologist Birgit Meyer,[16] in her book *Translating the Devil*, documents how early missionaries to the Ewe of Ghana translated Satan as *Abonsam*, an Akan term understood by the Ewe as a synonym for witch.

Meyer demonstrates how a translational process resulted in Ewe Christians interpreting the Christian message as ratifying their witch assumptions and attributions, and where a wide variety of words for evil used in Christian discourse are simply assumed to be "about witches." Because of this translation history, and according to her data, every time Satan is referenced, Ewe Christians hear a biblical affirmation that "witches are real." But even where translations were not so egregious as to translate Satan as witch,

---

14. Bosch, *Problem of Evil in Africa*, 38–62.
15. Personal email from Dr. Harriet Hill, April 27, 2011.
16. Meyer, *Translating the Devil*.

a similar process was often at work. This process can be seen in the article, "Shakespeare in the Bush," by anthropologist Laura Bohannan[17] about her effort to tell the story of Hamlet to the Tiv. While the original story of Hamlet makes no reference to the witch idea, the Tiv understood all sorts of evils referenced in Hamlet as witch-inflected. The appearance of Hamlet's deceased father was decoded as either an "apparition" or "zombie"—both of which were understood by the Tiv as created by witches. Madness, drowning, and a variety of other evils referenced in Hamlet were culturally assumed to be caused by witches. Bohannan was disconcerted to find that her audience had decoded her story about Hamlet as a story filled with witches, and that this is why they liked her story. In a similar fashion, when the Christian message is communicated in cultures permeated by witch ontologies, the message, not surprisingly, is often decoded as a message about witches. This may indeed be part of Christianity's attraction. Although the Bible nowhere links demonization/demon possession to witches, for example, exorcism passages in the gospels are often read in societies stressing witch ontologies as providing instruction on how to combat witchcraft.

When translators render Exodus 22:18 using indigenous terms for gossip-based attributions of ultimate evil to a neighbor or relative, as when the Swahili Bible says "You shall not allow a woman-witch to live," people naturally find their own diagnosis ratified and their own impulse to treat such accused persons as serial murderers endorsed by God.

Missionaries not only faced biblical silence about witch ontologies, a history of mistranslation seemingly ratifying such ontologies, and their own translational challenges in new settings, but missionaries and local theologians also characteristically have failed to understand the ways in which witch ideologies have shifted under the influence of Christianity. In pre-Christian societies stressing witch ontologies, people were involved in a wide variety of magico-religious practices that were not thought of as evil or as connected with the figure of the evil witch/sorcerer. But often under Christianity all traditional magico-religious practices were reconfigured as evil[18] in ways that linked much of traditional culture to the image of the witch. Since the image of Satan did not exist prior to the presence of Christianity, some missionaries took the indigenous term for the high God and used this term for Satan, while borrowing words from other languages for

---

17. Bohannan, *Shakespeare in the Bush*, 28–33.
18. Bohannan, *Shakespeare in the Bush*, 28–33.

the Christian God as happened with the Lele.[19] One effect of such a translational move was to associate all dimensions of traditional culture with Satan. Global Pentecostalism has widely embraced the spiritual warfare ideas of European and American authors,[20] including the core idea influentially propagated by Kurt Koch[21] that all folk magic or religious practices involve the establishment of enduring and familial demonic ties. Any folk magico-religious practice is said to constitute a contract with the demonic. And because the image of the witch was central to evil, when all pre-Christian folk magico-religious practices, including marriage rites, were reconfigured as evil, many Christian communities came to associate anyone's use of such practices with their being a witch-killer, an association not there prior to the influence of Christianity. Increasingly in some regions all the evidence needed to accuse and convict anyone of being a witch is evidence that they have used any traditional magico-religious practice, even those actually intended purely to protect themselves from witches. This represents an enormous shift from witch ideologies in pre-Christian cultures, and contributes in the contemporary world to the intergenerational scapegoating of the elderly as witches/sorcerers.

It is worth noting that while interpersonal causal ontology cultures prior to contact with Christianity often framed witch power as in-born, innate, psychic, even unconsciously exercised, having no necessary connection either with explicit magical practices or with sentient spirits, under the influence of Christianity witch discourses have migrated away from attributions of psychic, magical, or unconscious exercise of power towards attributions of power self-consciously exercised through magico-religious practices and tied to Satan and contracts with the devil. The underlying interpersonal causal ontology structure remains intact, but is now justified in more explicitly Christian terms. In many regions of the world it is now Christianity, which provides cognitive authority and underpinnings to witch ontologies. The logic explaining how witches operate has been recast in more Christian terms now provides another layer of difficulty faced by Christian missionaries, pastors, or theologians wishing to arrive at an adequately accurate understanding of what such discourses actually entail. Instead of encountering witch ideologies as pagan and non-Christian

---

19. Douglas, "Sorcery Accusations."
20. Onyinah, *Deliverance; Contemporary 'Witchdemonology' in Africa*, 330–45.
21. Ellis, *Raising the Devil*.

ideology, increasingly one encounters it as Christian. It is often Christians and pastors who are carriers of this ideology.

When interpersonal causal ontologies blame sinful third parties for affliction, such ontologies in biblical terms both go too far, and not far enough. They go too far in asserting that such human wishes are supernaturally efficacious.[22] They fail to go far enough in recognizing that it is not merely a few people who wish evil of others—but that this is a universal human condition shared by accusers and accused alike. It is this failure that underpins witch ontologies as scapegoating systems. Space precludes a full treatment of scapegoating, of Satan as accuser, Christ as the only truly innocent scapegoat who breaks the power of scapegoating, the Holy Spirit as paraclete and defender against all scapegoating accusers, including Satan the ultimate accuser.

Many western Christians do worry, perhaps rightly, that they have been overly contaminated by enlightenment naturalism, and thus hesitate to be critical of any approach that so clearly affirms the reality of demonic power. Yet, Scripture itself appears to call for Christians to exercise critical judgment, as when the apostle Paul warns against endorsing gossip-based ideas about spiritual realities which he calls "old wives fables" (1 Tim 4:7). Or again, when Jeremiah reflects on folk notions of spiritual power and associated practices by surrounding nations in chapter 10, he insists that these "customs of the peoples are worthless" and that the people of God should not give credence to them. Furthermore, as I have mentioned above, the idea that a human third party may be blamed for harming others through evil occult means lacks any biblical support. Despite the very real dangers of ethnocentrism or naturalism, we must somehow organize sustained critical attention to witch discourses and associated practices as part of Christian faithfulness. Not all discourses of the demonic are appropriately grounded in biblical authority. This paper has argued not only that such ideas fail to find any biblical support, but that the very ideas themselves contribute to suffering in our world.

Witch discourses (and accompanying reactions) result in great suffering in our world today. Christianity is positioned, in much of the world, as accrediting and providing intellectual underpinnings for witch discourses and accompanying practices, with social consequences to the accused. We therefore have a solemn responsibility to mobilize the effort to rethink our

---

22. While Scripture does present a world of evil supernatural beings that cause affliction, the agency for such affliction is not human.

role in this. We must not lend our authority to interpersonal causal ontologies, which lack biblical support. In my opinion, missiologists have not yet done an adequate job of wisely engaging these realities. We also have a significant opportunity, because, unlike western naturalists (who may lack any point of contact with those affirming witch realities), we do speak within the framework of a Christian supernaturalism.

Like the Boston ministers in Salem, Christian theologians and church leaders today have great potential to shape the direction of Christian thought and practice in this area, for good or ill. This effort to grapple with the issues must be done by an international community of anthropologists, missiologists, historians, and theologians. No analysis that ignores the social dynamics, especially as they relate to the accused, will be adequate. Insofar as witch accusations involve scapegoating of vulnerable people innocent of the charges, Christians must move from the activity of endorsing scapegoating accusations to the activity of paraclete, advocate and protector.

2

Navigating The Cross-Cultural Dynamics of Global Mission Organizations

An Interdisciplinary Approach

DONNA R. DOWNES

Introduction

Learning about Multicultural Mission the Hard Way

At the end of our seventh year in Kenya as missionaries, our multicultural "dream team" was in trouble. Our Kenyan team leader was disgusted with our mission agency which he called "imperialist and colonialist." Another Kenyan teammate complained about our team's questionable financial policies and lack of trust for Africans while an Ethiopian team member began searching for a new organization that would, he said, "truly appreciate his giftedness." A second Ethiopian was accusing the North American team members of dangerously meddling in family matters they did not understand. Within a short period of time, all our African teammates left the mission. What was once the model experiment of multicultural teamwork within our organization had become an embarrassment. How could a group of 15 multicultural missionaries dedicated to serving the Lord of the Harvest and to expanding the Kingdom of God together get it all so wrong? Indeed, what exactly had gone wrong, and how could we fix it so that God's name could be proclaimed through the multicultural witness of His people from every nation to every nation?

These questions drove my inquiries in applied research as I entered my doctoral studies. The insights gained from Lingenfelter's adaptation[1] of Mary Douglas's grid/group theory[2] began my journey in a helpful direction. Along the way, I encountered several other theoretical frameworks or lenses that amplified the use of Lingenfelter's model and led to the following conviction: Mission leaders ministering in partnership cross-culturally require a multidisciplinary understanding of leadership and organizational dynamics that can adjust and adapt to complex local and global cultural, educational, social, economic, and political change. Without such a broad understanding, mission leaders will continue to operate in personal or corporate "prison of disobedience."[3] This multidisciplinary understanding includes insights from the fields of anthropology, communications, missiology, leadership development, and international management.

Surveying the Landscape Then and Now

In 2001, when I conducted extensive survey research about the levels and types of globalization in North American mission organizations, results showed that very little structural or leadership change had taken place to accommodate or facilitate the growing impact of the non-North American missions movement around the world.[4] Since then, however, there has been much evidence that missionary structures (at least in North America) have been changing rapidly in light of new global mission realities.[5] Several North American-founded missionary structures no longer have a North American-based headquarters, but have developed instead what some are calling a "global alliance" with regional-level or national organizations agreeing to work together on the basis of a unifying statement of mission, vision and values. Each entity has equal stature and autonomy to make decisions regarding ministry strategy and evaluation, recruiting, training, missionary deployment, funding, and personnel development. But each entity also has a unifying corporate identity (an alliance) for sharing vision,

1. Lingenfelter, *Agents of Transformation*; *Transforming Culture*.
2. Douglas, *Cultural Bias*.
3. Lingenfelter, *Transforming Culture*, 16.
4. Downes, *Globalization of Mission*.
5. Dean, "Global Alliances."

funding, research information, ministerial expertise, strategies, training materials and other resources.[6]

Other organizations continue to explore multiple types of partnerships where mission organizations and/or churches agree to work together globally or locally on specific, time-bound objectives without the added requirement of organizational membership.[7] Even denominational missionary structures like the Christian Reformed Church and the Presbyterian Church (USA), which demonstrated almost no movement toward structural or leadership globalization in my initial survey, have in recently moved toward promoting global partnerships and greater involvement of non-North Americans in strategic leadership positions.[8] In addition to these more formal types of partnerships and alliances, the rapid growth of creative strategies for business as mission and bi-vocational ministries has added still another level of complexity to what it means to partner cross-culturally, especially in restricted access countries. Indeed, the structural landscape of global missions today is remarkably different from just a decade ago.[9]

Missions historian Dana Roberts has characterized the new global mission environment this way:

> With globalization we've now got a matrix of movement in which mission is taking place. . . . Mission is taking place through migration, for example, of people from Africa moving to Europe or to the United States, people from Latin America moving to the United States, people from the United States moving to Asia. The emphasis is not as much on the professional missionary who is sent from one place to another for a lifetime. It's a much more free-flowing set of networked relationships.
>
> Interest in mission is now bubbling up from the grass roots. The creativity that's flowing upward creates a state of chaos. It's much harder for a leader to stay on top of all of this, and a question is,

---

6. Several aspects of globalizing mission organizational structures and procedures have been discussed by OM (or "Operation Mobilization") leadership personnel in a series of publications available online. The publications reviewed for this article include: Nicoll, "Globalization and International Mission"; Lundy, "Moving Beyond," 147–55.

7. Audéoud and Pohor, "Hope for the Christian Church." See also a series of three articles by Livingood, "Global Partnering Growing Pains," 1–3.

8. Gravelle, "Mission Reinvention," 5–6. See also Wickeri, *Partnership, Solidarity, and Friendship*.

9. Priest, *New Era of Mission*, 294–304.

should a leader try to control it? Our structures need to move from controlling structures to enabling structures.[10]

However, despite the organizational movements over the last decade encouraging structural changes that accommodate and facilitate globalization of mission, Christian leaders still face major challenges in navigating the complexities of cross-cultural ministry. In other words, improving structure alone does not resolve all the issues related to the globalization of mission. Indeed, dozens of articles and books continue to be written on other challenges in global missions (e.g., multicultural conflict resolution, negotiating power, dealing with money problems, equalizing employee benefits, etc.).[11] While the complexities of mission in today's global context challenge Christian leaders are challenged by the, leaders today can also be resourced through a wide variety of interdisciplinary theory and models that may lighten their burdens, broaden their perspectives, and provide new insights on global leadership. In this chapter I briefly outline five of these theoretical perspectives, all of which I have used in my research and teaching and which have added immensely to my understanding of the cross-cultural dynamics of global missions.

The Contribution of Anthropology to Multicultural Missions

From the middle of the twentieth century when the academic discipline of missiology was born, to the present day, the field of anthropology has always figured significantly in the educational programs of missionaries. Anthropologists such as William Smalley, Eugene Nida, Alan Tippett, Louis Lutzbetak, Paul Hiebert, and Charles Kraft introduced thousands of missionaries to the usefulness of anthropology theory for the missionary endeavor.[12] As Christian anthropologist Eugene Nida once wrote, "Good missionaries have always been good 'anthropologists.' . . . Effective missionaries have always sought to immerse themselves in a profound knowledge of the ways of life of the people to whom they have sought to minister."[13] But while most of the written works of missionary anthropologists have

---

10. Roberts, "Missions in a Matrix."

11. See, for example, Lederleitner, *Cross-Cultural Partnerships*; Corwin, "Of Partnerships and Power Trips."

12. Whiteman, "Anthropology and Mission."

13. Nida, *Customs and Cultures*, ix.

concentrated on understanding the cultural dynamics of various ethnolinguistic groups around the world and on helping missionaries learn how to appreciate, love and live among people who were different from themselves. The anthropology of organizational culture has received little attention. This is indeed unfortunate, as cross-cultural teams often face unexpected conflict with colleagues over policies and practices that reflect monocultural rather than multicultural values.

Sherwood Lingenfelter, in his important book *Agents of Transformation*[14] departs from the traditional studies of anthropology in mission by demonstrating how his grid/group theory can illumine organizational settings, explaining how the dynamics of cultural values impact organizational values and behaviors. In the case study "Union Limited" (a case based on this author's own organizational research), Lingenfelter and Downes describe how deeply held African tribal values about family and community authority, property ownership, conflict, and labor interests can cause multiple misunderstandings in an organizational context, even when North American and African missionaries all were exposed to the same training about organizational culture.[15] For example, the purchase of property for a mission office and others acreage for individual agricultural use was an extremely high value among African teammates because "the ownership of land and the placement of buildings upon that land ... show a great deal of status in and identification with the community."[16] Although official mission policy discouraged the purchase of land in a foreign country because of tax and ownership issues with its not-for-profit status of registration in the United States, African team members insisted that the organization would not be seen as legitimate until such a long-term investment was made. Similarly, the Kenyan team members all owned land in rural areas as well as in the city because land constituted their social identity. Such was not simply a transactional resource, which was more the case with the other partners. North Americans viewed land with utilitarian lenses from their "low grid" orientation, while their Kenyan teammates viewed land from a "high grid" orientation as essential to community status and authority.[17] Land ownership and maintenance was a constant source of contention in the team.

14. Lingenfelter, *Agents of Transformation*.
15. Downes in Lingenfelter, *Agents of Transformation*, 54.
16. Lingenfelter, *Agents of Transformation*, 57.
17. Lingenfelter, *Agents of Transformation*, 57.

Another example of such conflict resulted from the organization's differing cultural values placed on "team." African teammates tended to view "team" from a high group perspective, a family collective with imperatives of trust, personal identity, and unquestionable commitment. North Americans saw team from a lower group perspective, a utilitarian workgroup drawn together by ministry vision and objectives. For African teammates, disagreements about policies and practices, therefore, often became questions of trust and personal identity. Alternately, North Americans frequently viewed such questions as open discussion forums for resolving conflict where discussions were measured against goals and objectives, and a high priority was placed upon resolution for the sake of work effectiveness.

The application of Lingenfelter's grid/group theoretical framework yielded wonderful insights into the source of team conflicts, but did not offer too much assistance in the practical resolution of those conflicts—especially interpersonal problems. For such resolution, this researcher turned to the area of intercultural communication and how that discipline might offer more than simply diagnosis.

The Contribution of Cross-Cultural Communications Theory in Multicultural Missions

It is common knowledge among cross-cultural communication experts that the vast majority of human communication lay not in what is actually said but what is communicated contextually and nonverbally (often unintentionally) through our physical environment, our gestures, our tone of voice, eye contact, facial expression, proximity, and several other "signal systems."[18] In fact, one of the bestselling and most popular university textbooks on intercultural communication features a single chapter on language and culture. The remainder of the over 400-page text is devoted to the nonverbal contextual elements (history, religion, values and social organizations) that impact human understanding of what is actually said.[19]

One of the first communications specialists to recognize the importance of nonverbal communications in an organizational environment was Edward T. Hall, author of *The Hidden Dimension*, still popular today after

---

18. Smith, *Creating Understanding*.

19. Samovar et al., *Communication Between Cultures*. Only in chapter 6, with a mere twenty-one pages, do the authors deal specifically with language, and even that is discussed in terms of context (Samovar et al., *Communication Between Cultures*, 177–212).

six decades in publication.[20] In humorous but sobering ways, Hall compares what the proxemics and manipulation of space communicates cross-culturally in German, English and French corporate offices. Little did this author realize that twenty years after reading this book in college, the reality of proxemics would become a critical element in miscommunications among missionary teammates in Kenya. In that context, North American "low grid" values of utilitarian office space allocation became highly offensive to the "higher grid" Africans whose choice of office space (ground floor or upper floors, shared or individual) communicated the status of the person in that office. While both African and North American teammates were not seeking offices solely as status symbols, several feared what would be communicated to the community of church leaders if office space were not allocated in a culturally acceptable way.

While almost all the elements of nonverbal communication became points of contention or discussion in this author's missionary experience in Kenya, none were as important as the manner in which conflicts were resolved. Toward this end, the work of cross-cultural expert and educator Duane Elmer contributed greatly. Again, from the knowledge first gained through Lingenfelter's grid/group theory, this author asked questions about conflict resolution styles in a high-grid and high-group context. Elmer's concepts about indirect conflict resolution, mediation, storytelling and proverbs, vulnerability and the "one-down" position helped the team to view conflict from the perspective of resolution rather than the precise method used to reach that resolution. The biblical concept of conflict resolution in Matthew 18 took on new meaning as we began to appreciate the cross-cultural nuances of what it means to confront (with love and care) a brother or sister who offended us.

One early researcher in discipline of cross-cultural management is Dutch sociologist Geert Hofstede. In the 1970s and 1980s, Hofstede introduced major multinational businesses (especially IBM) to the importance of local culture on corporate management practices. His detailed study of the cultural traits of forty countries was first published in 1980 and since then has been rewritten several times to accommodate new data for additional countries. His recent 2010 edition of his popular book *Cultures and Organizations*, now lists cultural values data for 107 countries or regions,[21] with many researchers now adding to the bank of information

---

20. Hall, *Hidden Dimension*.
21. Hofstede et al., *Cultures and Organizations*, 36.

already available. Hofstede originally posited four cultural "dimensions" that greatly influence the day-to-day environment of corporations doing business cross-culturally.[22]

1. *Power distance*-the degree to which the less powerful members of a society accept and expect that power is distributed unequally.
2. *Individualism vs. collectivism*-society's position about whether people define their self-image in terms of "I" or "we," and the degree to which individuals expect to take care of themselves vs. their obligation to take care of an extended family or community.
3. *Masculinity vs. Femininity*-masculinity represents a preference in society for achievement, heroism, assertiveness and material reward for success, which produces a society, or culture that is competitive. Its opposite, femininity, stands for a preference for cooperation, modesty, caring for the weak and quality of life.
4. *Uncertainty Avoidance*-the degree to which the members of a society feel uncomfortable with uncertainty and ambiguity. The fundamental issue here is how a society deals with the fact that the future can never be known. Such involves whether people try to control the future or just let it happen.

In the last decade, Hofstede has added to his original work two cultural dimensions.[23]

1. *Short vs. Long-term Orientation*–this explains Chinese Confucian values and a "society's search for virtue." Those with a short-term orientation generally possess a strong concern with establishing the absolute Truth and doing so quickly; those that operate with a longer-term orientation believe that truth depends very much on situation, context and time.
2. *Indulgence vs. Restraint*–this dimension relates to how cultures place value upon enjoying life and having fun vs. the suppression of such gratification because of certain social norms and expectations.

While Hofstede's work is often criticized for conflating social values and stereotyping them into "national cultural dimensions" (as if an entire country could be defined according to one set of cultural values), the

22. Hofstede, "National Culture Dimensions."
23. Hofstede, "National Culture Dimensions."

Devoted to Christ

simplicity of his categorization and the plentiful examples of how the values are manifested in organizational culture make his research readily understandable and acceptable to business people worldwide. In this researcher's experience, Hofstede's work on the dimension of individualism vs. collectivism helped greatly to explain the immense responsibility our African teammates felt for their extended families, to family land, and to their family reputation. The North Americans on the team felt that such strong dedication to collectivist values sometimes got in the way of corporate responsibilities to fulfill organizational goals and objectives. For our African teammates, getting "Aunt Mary's" children into the best boarding schools, for example, sometimes took greater priority over planning for the next pastor's conference.

The Contribution of Diversity Management Theory to Leveraging Cultural Differences in Multicultural Missions

One of the more controversial fields in organizational leadership today is diversity management where the units of analysis are the organizational structure, day-to-day practices and the overall culture. Each element is evaluated as to how it either discourages and impedes or encourages and promotes diversity. In this field of study, "diversity" is not restricted to cultural diversity, but includes gender, racial, religious, and economic diversity as well. For the purposes of my own doctoral research, cultural diversity became the central focus. One of the early writers in this field was diversity management consultant, Taylor Cox, Jr. whose 1991 article in the *Academy of Management Executive* marked the beginning of several books and articles contributing to the field.[24] Cox identifies six dimensions by which organizations must analyze and improve their diversity practices:

1. The appreciation of cultural pluralism and the creation of an environment where minority cultural voices and perspectives can positively influence organizational norms and values
2. Structural Integration (the ability to conform organizational structure to encourage and enable organizational diversity)
3. Integration of cultural diversity into informal social networks

---

24. Cox, "Multicultural Organization," 34–47.

4. Eliminating cultural discrimination and prejudice through in-service training, proactive recruitment and advancement policies, and ongoing research and evaluation.
5. Organizational identification and image which publicly promotes a positive view of diversity.
6. Resolution of Intergroup Conflict where efforts are made to handle conflict in a balanced way.[25]

In his 2001 book, *Creating the Multicultural Organization*, Cox also stressed the importance of the leaders' commitment to recognizing, cultivating and appreciating the positive contribution of diverse voices and cultural views to an organization's success.[26]

How did diversity theory help our troubled Kenyan team and our mission organization as a whole? Earlier I quoted one of our African teammates who labeled our mission organization as "imperialist and colonialist" in its culture and practices. His statement caused leaders in the mission to analyze and change several aspects of our organization's culture that inhibited diversity. These included the use of "English" as our *lingua franca* for conferences and strategic meetings (which discouraged full participation of those for whom spoken English is weak), the centralization of training geographically in America (which favored North American participants), the setting of financial support requirements at North American levels (which discouraged international recruitment), health insurance requirements that are based on medical care in the USA (the practicality and cost of which was prohibitive to non-USA citizens), and the practice of recruiting US-seminary graduates (which inhibits the engagement of missionaries prepared and sent by churches and organizations in other nations). These are just a few of the policies and practices that discouraged diversity and inhibited full participation of non-North Americans in the mission. The contributions of others in the field of diversity management continue to provide new insights into areas where mission organizations might improve.[27] As Gary Corwin reminds us, mission leaders must always "resist diversity as a goal, but embrace it as a means." Corwin explains, "God has

---

25. Cox, "Multicultural Organization," 34–47.

26. Cox, *Creating the Multicultural Organization*, 33–58.

27. Newer works on diversity management include Patrick and Kumar, "Managing Workplace Diversity"; Moran et al., *Managing Cultural Differences*; Barak, *Managing Diversity*.

larger issues he wants us to address, but he wants us to do it the way he does things, by celebrating and benefiting from the diverse and uniquely valuable resources he has provided."[28]

The Contribution from Organizational Dynamics in encouraging Flexibility and Creativity in Multicultural Mission

One of the most popular management textbooks over the past three decades is Bolman's and Deal's creative volume on organizational leadership entitled *Reframing Organizations*.[29] The authors suggest that every organization (in both the private and nonprofit sectors) deals with problems or challenges from one of four basic values-oriented approaches or frameworks. First is the *"structural"* approach where problems are most often addressed by adjusting organizational charts, adding new departments or levels of accountability, dealing with goals and objectives and job descriptions, etc. The authors write:

> Structures—commonly depicted by organization charts—are designed to fit an organization's environment and technology. . . . They then create rules, policies, procedures, systems, and hierarchies to coordinate diverse activities into a unified effort. Problems arise when structure doesn't line up well with current circumstances. At that point, some form of reorganization or redesign is needed to remedy the mismatch.[30]

Second, the authors identify the *human resources approach* where people are the central focus of an organization's operations. In this type of organizational culture, problems will be minimized if the people are treated well, attention is given to individual "needs, feelings, prejudices, skills and limitations," and they feel their voices are heard and appreciated. Bolman and Deal write: "From a human resources view, the key challenge is to tailor organizations to individuals—finding ways for people to get the job done while feeling good about themselves and their work."[31] Common elements of the human resources approach are an emphasis on personnel enrichment

---

28. Corwin, "Doing Diversity Well," 417.
29. Bolman and Deal, *Reframing Organizations*.
30. Bolman and Deal, *Reframing Organizations*, 15–16.
31. Bolman and Deal, *Reframing Organizations*, 16.

programs, leadership development, in-service training, employee satisfaction surveys, etc.

Third, organizations can manifest a *political framework* where organizations are seen as "arenas, contests, or jungles" where "parochial interests compete for power and scarce resources." Conflict arises when too much power is concentrated in one position or person or when people do not feel they have the necessary resources to do their jobs. The authors write:

> Bargaining, negotiation, coercion, and compromise are a normal part of everyday life. Coalitions are formed around specific interests and change as issues come and go. Problems arise when power is concentrated in the wrong place or is so broadly dispersed that nothing gets done. Solutions arise from political skill and acumen.[32]

While many Christian organizations might object to the morality of allowing a political framework to function in Christian ministries, when resources are scarce and only certain programs or people can be funded, the political framework often becomes very prominent.

Forth, the authors write about the *symbolic framework* where organizations are seen "as cultures, propelled by rituals, ceremonies, stories, heroes, and myths rather than rules, policies, and managerial authority."[33] Usually these organizations have a strong historic narrative, visual symbols, and frequent celebrations or rituals that pull people together for a particular cause. Problems arise when the rituals lose their meaning, when history becomes tarnished, or when key charismatic leaders fail. The solution to problems is often an effort at reimaging the organization and creating new culture, ritual and celebration.

The authors conclude their text by urging leaders to become adept at using of each of the frameworks to identify and deal with problems as they arise. They write: "Leaders fail when they take too narrow a view. Unless they can think flexibly and see organizations from multiple angles, they will be unable to deal with the full range of issues they inevitably encounter."[34]

While Bolman and Deal do not apply their four frameworks specifically to cross-cultural contexts, this author began to question whether certain types of management frames would be more or less effective in facilitating multicultural teamwork. In Kenya, for example, where a high group,

32. Bolman and Deal, *Reframing Organizations*, 16.
33. Bolman and Deal, *Reframing Organizations*, 16.
34. Bolman and Deal, *Reframing Organizations*, 437.

collectivist orientation governed the participation of our African colleagues in the organization's ministry, the symbolic, historic and celebratory approach to organizational leadership became a valuable solution for pulling the team together around a common identity, vision, organizational history and set of missionary values. The celebration of organizational milestones, answered prayers, and individual accomplishments became a regular and frequent ritual for the team and the practice helped to ameliorate conflicts and to build a new cooperative team culture. In the same vein, when problems occurred that required structural and policy changes, it was good to be able to recognize that fact and make the necessary adjustments (such as those areas mentioned above in the section on diversity theory).

Navigating the Complexities of Globalization Together for the Sake of the Kingdom

At the end of his book *Leading Cross-Culturally*, Lingenfelter reminds us clearly that no matter what methods or modern theories we attempt to apply to help us in cross-cultural ministry, our first priority is to be obedient disciples of Christ. He writes:

> When we worship and live in obedience to the King of kings, God transforms leaders, teams, and every form of social game into covenant communities, called out for the mission of God and working together in unity to fulfill their divine purpose. When we worship at the cross, we learn to take the path of weakness rather than of power, to extend mutual forgiveness rather than condemnation, and to submit to one another rather than seeking power and the subjection of others to our will in our relationships and teamwork.[35]

The road will not be easy since we are human and we all operate out of our own cultural "prisons of disobedience."[36] But God has made it possible to break free of that prison when we learn to appreciate our differences and to see them as part of God's creative genius in expanding His Kingdom around the world. The creative, combined wisdom that God has given us through a multiplicity of disciplines, as shown in this article, serves only to exemplify the fact that finding our way through the labyrinth of globalization requires sharing resources, power, and insights across cultures and continents. At

35. Lingenfelter, *Leading Cross-Culturally*, 170.
36. Lingenfelter, *Transforming Culture*, 16.

the Lausanne Cape Town gathering in 2010, such a commitment became the rallying point of the entire missions community:

> We stand together as church and mission leaders in all parts of the world, called to recognize and accept one another, with equality of opportunities to contribute together to world mission. Let us, in submission to Christ, lay aside suspicion, competition and pride and be willing to learn from those whom God is using, even when they are not from our continent, nor of our particular theology, nor of our organization, nor of our circle of friends.[37]

---

37. Lausanne Movement, "Confession of Faith."

3

The State of Minority Languages in the Twenty-First Century

In praise of language, in search of compassion

JOHN R. WATTERS

Introduction

Language and *culture* refers to two closely bound realities of human existence. Every human culture is identified with at least one human language, whether spoken or signed. Every human language allows for a far greater understanding of its associated culture than simply observing cultural behavior without language. Language provides a window on the thoughts, emotions, perceptions, and motivations of the individuals within that culture. Some might claim that the relationship between the two is a symbiotic (two dissimilar realities in intimate relationship). Others might claim it is organic (two realities forming a larger integral relationship). Neither can exist without the other, regardless of which adjective best describes the relationship.

In this article, I move across the aisle to discuss culture's well-weathered friend, namely, human language, whether spoken or signed.[1] I focus

1. Sherwood Lingenfelter—as a professor of anthropology with expertise in social structure, leadership, culture change, and cross-cultural partnership—has brought anthropology and the study of culture to bear in significant ways on issues of cross-cultural life for SIL International and its personnel. Whether it involves serving, teaching, or

particularly on the status of the lesser-known languages of the world. Ultimately the goal is to reflect on certain realities concerning the lesser-known languages of the world and their implications for language development, education and translation programs in the communities that speak these languages. In this article I refer to such as 'minority languages' spoken by 'minority language communities.' I will comment further on the use of the term 'minority' below.

Here I argue that as a matter of equity, justice, ethics and compassion, minority language communities and their languages deserve greater authentic attention and investment of resources in national and regional plans and programs. The goal is to increase the probability that their languages can sustainably serve the needs and goals of the community of speakers in the current and coming generations.

The term 'minority language' may come across to some as a negative or even pejorative descriptor for these languages. That is not, however, the intent. The term is used to reflect the actual socio-psychological experience of speakers of these languages. Minority language speakers know their languages have value, but that is not the message they often receive from governments and other entities with power to impact their lives. They rarely find speakers of the dominant language in their region marveling at the wonder of their language. We could refer to such languages as 'lesser known languages' but that might imply that others in dominant, majority languages might actually want to know (about) their languages, which is far from the case[2]. Their languages are usually ignored, treated with benign neglect, or even viewed with contempt and hostility from speakers of dominant languages and those in dominant power structures. The phrases 'minority language' and 'minority language community' are fitting descriptors

---

leading cross-culturally in ways that seek to honor God and honor the 'other' across the cultural boundary, he has applied the genius of the British anthropologist Mary Douglas (1982) and her social variables of grid and group to the contexts in which the activities of serving, teaching or leading take place. The observations offered here regarding language and "minority language communities" serve as a small counterpart compared to Lingenfelter's ample thoroughgoing cultural insights. My hope is that some of these observations may provide new perspectives or more nuanced understandings of the issues surrounding these communities.

2. This article reflects my experience with one such language and language community in Cameroon and Nigeria, as well as my interactions with individuals from 'minority language communities' across Africa, Asia, Central America, Europe, South America and the Pacific Islands. These communities generally share a common experience relative to dominant languages and national or regional decision-makers.

of these communities' experience relative to whatever culture and language is dominant in their region or nation. What this means for a given minority language will vary and depend on its linguistic context.

The status of minority languages should be a topic of significant concern to many entities-government institutions responsible for education, non-governmental organizations involved in community development projects, churches that claim to include individuals from every tribe and language, and all organizations involved in communicating important life-changing knowledge. At times, those who speak minority languages are blamed for failure of their children in school, for failure of development projects in their region, or the failure of a community to understand what is being communicated to them in the language of wider communication. The assigned fault is frequently attributed to their dependence on their minority language. It is as if these communities have to take the responsibility to uproot themselves from their inherited identity, forget their language, and adopt the language of wider communication as their own. In fact, the serving organizations may be culpable because they have not made the appropriate effort to step into the linguistic world of the minority community even though they are usually resource-rich relative to the minority community.

The wonder and uniqueness of human language

Most people are curious about language since it is an integral part of their daily lives. They are particularly aware of language when they hear someone speaking a different language. One of the wonders is that each of us uses language every day in virtually all aspects of our lives. We use the extraordinary ability of speaking and understanding others speak without thinking or reflecting on it. It is taken for granted like breathing. The words (or signs for those that use signed language) simply flow from our mouths (or signs from our hands and bodies) in situation after situation without much thought about how it works.

I will affirm the facts that language is unique to human beings, that its foundational principles are shared by all human languages, and that the innovative capacity to create new languages based on those principles is resident in humans. We will note the centrality of human language in all aspects of human knowledge, community life and identity.

To refer to human language as "unique" will raise questions and concerns in certain circles. It may seem to fly in the face of various questionable attempts to define humankind by specific, unique, identifiable traits. This process of identifying the uniqueness of human beings has been a troubled enterprise. Beginning with the assertion that humankind differs from other animals as tool-makers and continuing to assertions over possible unique traits such as aggression, empathy, and culture, each so-called unique trait has been questioned and often ultimately undermined. Many argue that any difference is really one of magnitude rather than a difference in kind and so do not uniquely distinguish humans from animals.

Over the past decades, specialists in animal studies have attempted to reduce or even erase the accepted gap between humans and animals. Such seek to demonstrate that these differences are of degree rather than kind. At the same time, it seems clear that various animals have unique capacities that work well for them within their niche in the biological world. These unique capacities seem to distinguish them from human beings. For example, birds possess wings that provide them with the capacity to fly, fish have gills that allow them to stay underwater without ever coming to the surface to breathe, bats have sonar capabilities to find food in the dark, and dogs have exceptional ability to smell. Given their unique capacity for language humans gain knowledge of the world and pass that knowledge on from one generation to the next. They can do so not because they can fly or swim or use sonar or smell across great distances, but because they possess the unique capacity of language.

Language as a phenomenon of human behavior is of interest to scientists and so is subject to scientific description, explanation and speculation. What linguists are saying about language certainly underscores the extraordinary nature of this ability. As would be expected, most scientific interest in language flourishes among linguists. Linguists seek to describe and explain the variety of complex structures and processes found in individual languages and in human language in general. When they speak of "human language in general," they are often referring to what some might call "Universal Grammar" or others might refer to as "universals." Linguists most often study details of language that are not well understood by those outside the linguistic academic community.

However, linguists as well as non-linguists are also interested in other questions about language. For those concerned with research of the human mind, the study of language provides a window on the structure and processes of the brain. Those concerned with speculative pre-history of humans focus on the origins of human language. For those concerned with comparative biology, the focus revolves around the uniqueness or non-uniqueness of human language in comparison to the communication systems found among animals.

Three major questions that interest scientists and non-scientists alike regarding language include: 1) How does human language compare to animal communication systems? 2) What is the origin of human language? 3) Why are there so many different languages in the world? I will comment on these three in summary form by referring to comments from some leading scholars of linguistics as well as one psychologist who specializes in language issues.

The first question of how human language compares to animal communication systems recognizes that animals do in fact have communication systems. Whether primates, varieties of birds, dolphins, or various insects, communication systems are abundant in the animal world. Some are quite elaborate and use various means other than voice to communicate. However, humans alone use language.

Anderson[3] claims that what is unique about human language is syntax, a feature that does not appear in animal communication systems. Syntax involves more than putting words in a linear order to produce sentences or parts of sentences such as larger phrases out of single words. For example, the noun *bird* can be expanded into the noun phrase *the red bird*. This is certainly part of syntax. However, the "more" that syntax is about includes the capacity to produce acceptable syntactic structures within the given language and to retrieve the meaning of the sentence from its complex internal structure and its assigned lexical items. This meaning may not be immediately accessible simply from the linear order of the surface structure of the sentence. Consider the following two sentences from Anderson.[4]

> *John is eager to please.*
> *John is easy to please.*

On the surface, these sentences appear parallel in their structure. However, their underlying syntactic structures are quite different as are the composite meaning of the sentences. The lexical item 'eager' is different from the lexical item 'easy.' In the first sentence, John is the person who is eager. He

---

3. Anderson, *Doctor Dolittle's Delusion*.
4. Anderson, *Doctor Dolittle's Delusion*, 221.

is the agent and is the one who wants to do the pleasing. In the second sentence, John is the person who receives the pleasing. He is the patient. The agent is not stated but we know that whoever the agent is John can be pleased without much effort.

Alternatively, consider these sentences.

> Mary appreciated Tom.
> Tom is the person that someone said Mary appreciated.

On the surface, it is clear in the first sentence that Tom is the object of Mary's appreciation. 'Tom' immediately follows the verb 'appreciate' as one would expect for an object of the verb in English. In the second sentence, however, Tom does not follow the verb 'appreciate.' Instead, nothing follows the verb 'appreciate' and Tom occurs at the beginning of the sentence. Yet, any speaker of English knows that Tom is still the object of Mary's appreciation even though his name appears some distance from the verb. The verb 'appreciate' is embedded two clauses below the clause that contains 'Tom.' This ability to interpret who the object of the 'appreciate' is in the second sentence is another example of syntax at work. It is not just the order of the words that help us understand the sentence, but the complex internal structure as well. There are no known cases where animal communication systems provide such rich structure. These examples provide only a beginning sample. One of the features of structures in human languages is that they can be recursive. This means that structures can be embedded within structures, producing a communication system that is unbounded. Anderson summarizes this extraordinary feature of human language, noting that such "makes it possible to express a vast range of notions that have no analogue in animal communication systems."[5] The capacity to combine elements syntactically and semantically sets humans apart as the only species with what we can refer to as 'language'—something different from a 'communication system.' Therefore, language is unique to humans. Human language consists of complex structures that allow humans to produce and understand an indefinite number of novel utterances. There is no limit to the number of such utterances. No animal communication system provides such an open-ended possibility of producing an indefinite number of novel utterances.

---

5. Anderson, *Doctor Dolittle's Delusion*, 220. This conclusion is shared by other scholars who have written extensively on human language, e.g., Pinker, *Language Instinct*; Jackendoff, *Foundations of Language*; Bickerton, *Adam's Tongue*.

The second question involves the origin of human language. Not surprisingly, it is here that the answers become highly speculative since little physical data exists. Writing came into use about 5,000 years ago, relegating all claims regarding the development of human language before that date as uncertain. The answers that are provided to this question assume different evolutionary theories[6] or are skeptical about a possible theory to explain its nature (e.g., Noam Chomsky,[7] who is satisfied to state simply that language is "innate"). As Anderson[8] notes, the fossil record does not provide data because the apparatus that produces oral language is composed of soft tissue. This would include the larynx, velum, tongue and brain. Since soft tissue does not usually survive over time, the physical fossil record cannot provide data to help answer this question.

Another direction to look is that of comparative analysis. For example, by comparing the communication of bats, dolphins, and chimps with that of humans it is possible to determine whether there exists a shared type of communication, or whether they are significant differences of kind between them. It is in this type of analysis that the distinction becomes apparent: whether spoken or signed language, the use of syntax is not found among any other species. Humans alone possess this trait.[9]

The third question involves the number of different languages in the world. Pinker[10] summarizes that differences in the numbers of languages are due to three processes: innovation, learning, and migration. The first involves the creative aspect of human language. Humans can innovate in human language in a variety of ways, from changing the sounds they use to changing the vocabulary to changing the syntax and meaning of words. Changes such as these can gradually become so significant that what were once two dialects of the same language become two separate, mutually unintelligible languages. Second is the issue of learning. Children learn to speak from their parents. In the process, they learn the innovations that their parents' generation and previous generations made. At birth, humans do not revert to some original form of language. The form of a language

---

6. Pinker, *Language Instinct*; Jackendoff, *Foundations of Language*; Bickerton, *Adam's Tongue*.

7. See Chomsky, *Syntactic Structures*.

8. Pinker, *Language Instinct*; Jackendoff, *Foundations of Language*; Bickerton, *Adam's Tongue*.

9. See Watters, "Syntax," for an introduction to syntax in African languages.

10. Watters, "Syntax," 243.

like English or Chinese is not hardwired in the brain but learned from the older generation. What are hardwired are general principles that all languages, including English and Chinese, are built upon. Third, migration can lead to isolation of language communities. They can become isolated geographically, religiously, socially, and so on. Without contact with related languages, speakers are freer to innovate without reference to their neighbors or speakers of related languages. Therefore, we see that humans have the capacity to modify their language and make it increasingly less intelligible to those outside the community. This relates to the difficulty that exists in distinguishing languages from dialects since there is often no clear demarcation between the two but instead what is often found are gradual, graded boundaries between the different speech forms that are continuing to change and differentiate over time.

To summarize, scientists claim that language is unique to human beings. All human languages share a common foundation and origin. This allows for the study of universals across languages and the possibility of translation from one language to another. Human language is dynamic and open to innovation, which leads to dialects becoming differentiated as distinct languages when the dialects are no longer mutually intelligible. This differentiation leads to the great number of languages that humans speak today and have spoken in the past.

The centrality of language

Scientific, educational, and religious perspectives all affirm the centrality of language. Bickerton[11] begins his introduction to the origin and centrality of language by writing that "Language is what makes us human. Maybe it's the only thing that makes us human." He points out that without language there would not be 'great problems' to ponder and discuss. The greatest problems in science can only be posed or addressed by using language. We could add that the same goes with the greatest questions of life. None of the great questions about what is true, good and beautiful would be possible without language.

From an educational perspective, Javier Pérez de Cuellar,[12] a previous Director-General of UNESCO, argues for investing in the local language of

---

11. Bickerton, *Adam's Tongue*.
12. De Cuéllar, "Our Creative Diversity," 10–11.

the given community because it is fundamental to their culture and identity. Language in education becomes a central political challenge. He writes,

> One of the most sensitive issues is that of language, for a people's language is perhaps its most fundamental cultural attribute. Indeed the very nature of language is emblematic of the whole pluralistic premise—every single language spoken in the world represents a unique way of viewing human experience and the world itself . . . the question of how to accommodate minorities is not of academic interest only but is a central challenge to any human politics. . . . Indigenous languages continue to be the main medium of expression of aspirations, intimate desires, feelings and local life. They are indeed the living repositories of cultures.[13]

He adds that primary school should be the place where these minority languages are integrated into the educational system.

From a religious perspective, the Abrahamic religions of Judaism, Christianity and Islam all locate written, revelatory language as a foundational dimension of their faith. In the first chapter of Genesis, God speaks the universe and world into existence. Psalm 19:1–6 makes the metaphorical point that creation has a language that reflects back its glory on its Creator that spoke it into existence; verses 7–11 point to God making his will for humans accessible through language (including forms such as laws, statutes, precepts, commands, and ordinances) and verses 12–14 point to the language of the heart and conscience with the powerful thought that connects our thoughts to our words: "May the words of my mouth and the meditation of my heart be pleasing in your sight, O Lord, my Rock and my Redeemer."

In summary, human languages are unique in their use of syntax in comparison to animal communication systems. Syntax allows humans to produce and understand an indefinite number of novel utterances. All human languages share the same foundational principles and therefore a common origin. Human language allows human beings to build an indefinitely expanding knowledge base. Human languages are also central to human existence.

Science, culturally relevant primary education, and theological reflection on religious texts all provide examples of the centrality of language to human existence and identity. These affirmations emphasize the imperative

---

13. De Cuéllar, "Our Creative Diversity," 59.

for all human institutions to respect all human languages in the pursuit of their goals.

The status of minority languages and the communities that speak them

In contrast to the affirming perspective on human language I have developed, speakers of minority languages typically have a different experience. Instead of their languages being objects of wonder and value, they are often treated with indifference, even contempt and hostility by the majority language culture. This attitude easily carries over into institutions and the policies of their decision-makers. Whether government leaders, leaders of NGOs, leaders of churches or other religious institutions, the decision-makers have a great impact on the place of minority languages within national institutions.

In this section, I turn to the central question of this article, namely, the state of minority languages relative to the current global realities. The questions I explore here are the nature of minority languages and their communities in the twenty-first century and the implications for national institutions in nations with multiple languages spoken within their borders.

The term "minority language"

At this point, I wish to clarify the meaning of the term "minority language." The concept of 'minority languages' is associated with a number of attributes. First, it is a language with relatively few speakers. Table 1 uses data on the 7,097 living languages recorded in the 2016 Ethnologue.[14] They estimate the distribution of languages based upon number of speakers.

---

14. Lewis et al., *Ethnologue*.

Number of speakers	Number of languages	(%) of World Population
10 million or more	92	80.26
1 million to 9,999,999	306	14.10
100,000 to 999,999	944	4.57
10,000 to 99,999	1808	0.94
Fewer than 10,000	3738	0.12
Unknown	209	–

Table 1: Living languages, their number of speakers, and world population

In the sixteenth edition of the Ethnologue, Lewis noted that Table 1 shows a significant disparity between the mean size of languages and the median size.[15] 398 (or nearly 6 percent) of the world's languages have at least one million speakers and account for 94 percent of the world's population, while the remaining 94 percent of languages are spoken by only 6 percent of the world population." The median size of the world's languages is about 6,000 speakers, whereas the mean (or average) size is greater than 850,000 speakers.

'Minority languages' do not generally include those 92 languages listed as having more than 10 million speakers. They do generally include those 6,699 languages with fewer than 1 million. They also likely include a number of languages with more than 1 million speakers. Being a minority language depends on the context in which the language is spoken. Therefore, a language with 100 million speakers can easily dominate a language with only a few million speakers. Estimates place 20 percent of the world's population in the category of speaking a minority language. Overall, the minority languages of the world include the "bottom billion" brought to our attention by Collier.[16] Given these numbers it is easy to see how power and decision-making roles are concentrated largely in the hands of those coming from the 85 largest languages in the world.

A second attribute of a minority language is that it is often an unwritten language. Frequently, these have no standard alphabet or writing system. No government institution or other institution has invested in these language communities to assist them in developing their languages in written form.

---

15. Lewis et al., *Ethnologue*, 20.
16. Collier, *Bottom Billion*.

Third, they are often ignored or treated with benign neglect by most institutions. These languages have no official role in governmental, educational, religious or other institutions where a written language is required. In some nations, laws dating from the colonial era have existed that prohibited children from speaking minority languages on school grounds.

Fourth, besides the status of the languages and the number of their speakers, a constellation of other attributes defines these minority language communities. These include:

- Economics—most often among the poorest
- Medical—most often in the bottom 20 percent of those receiving service
- Political—most often among the most disenfranchised
- Social—most often among the least valued
- Education—most often among the least educated
- Justice-wise—most often among the least informed of their rights and privileges
- Human dignity—most often the least honored

An important fifth point is that minority language communities today exist in a very different world from that of their ancestors fifty, one hundred, or two hundred years ago. One hundred years ago, many minority languages could exist in isolation from the larger world. This was true in many places even 50 years ago. However, today very few language communities are isolated from the world's global economy and national political structures. Globalization is impacting most of them in a variety of ways.

The gap

Earlier, I noted how human language is unique and central to human beings in numerous ways. In particular, I mentioned three domains (scientific, educational and religious). Yet there is a significant portion of humanity that do not gain as fully as they could from the language they speak. They live on the margins of the larger society dominated by languages of wider communication and international languages. In terms of governments and society, this gap raises issues of social justice and equity. In terms of non-governmental organizations and religious organizations such as churches, it also raises issues of mercy and compassion. The speakers of these languages form the "bottom billion" of the world's population, if not more. It would appear that governments, educational institutions, non-governmental organizations, churches, as well as other institutions bear a significant responsibility in this issue. In each case, these institutions are often serving people from these communities but often do not give due attention to the language needs that remain unmet.

Currently SIL International is involved with about 1,600 minority languages. Over its 77-year history, SIL International's linguistic investigation has exceeded 2,600 languages, spoken by 1.7 billion people in nearly 100 countries. At the same time, there may be as many as 2,000 additional languages for which no alphabet has been designed or materials produced but which would benefit from the language development program. This remains a significant challenge for the world. When taking account of those languages that now have an alphabet and some materials but are still significantly underserved (by the governmental, non-governmental and religious institutions of the country), it is clear that the remaining work is significant.

Language endangerment, language development, and measuring language viability

What is the proper response to endangered languages given such a great need? The response is at least twofold. First, there has been a growing awareness over the past decades of the issue of language death. Second, there is a need for continuing assessment of languages. Both of these relate to the publishing of the *Ethnologue* and the identification and counting of languages.

As with the counting of anything, the object of counting needs to be identifiable. This requires certain assumptions or definitions as to what the object is. In the case of languages, various definitions are possible. A variation of definitions leads to variation in counts. For example, in the case of Bantu languages the counting of languages varies between 250 and 550.[17] Like so much else in the natural world, discrete boundaries between languages and neighboring languages are often difficult to draw. What some consider a dialect continuum others may term a language continuum. In some cases, a given language is clearly differentiated from other languages. In the case of the *Ethnologue*, two basic criteria are used. First, when

---

17. Nurse, *Tense and Aspect in Bantu*.

comparing two or more speech forms, the criterion of mutually intelligibility is used. Yet, even this criterion is variable from situation to situation, often with significant gradations. If it is concluded, however, that they cannot understand one another at a certain level, these are considered distinct languages, even if they happen to share a common linguistic heritage. So, for example, Frisian, the closest related Germanic language to English, and English would be considered two distinct languages because they are not mutually intelligible. Second, even if two speech forms are mutually intelligible, there may be sociolinguistic or socio-political issues that keep them from forming a single, unified linguistic unit. In this case, they would be considered separate languages.

Based on these criteria of mutual intelligibility and sociolinguistic attitudes, the 2000 *Ethnologue* identified 6,809 languages.[18] Of the 6,809 languages the *Ethnologue* identified, there were 413 languages nearing extinction, and an additional 421 languages likely not viable. These 834 languages were more than 12 percent of the languages recorded in the *Ethnologue*. This means that nearly 1 out of 8 languages in the world would likely never benefit from a full language development, educational, or translation project. They could still benefit from linguistic documentation and research, and in some cases, special projects could be developed for the last generation or two speaking the given language.

On the other hand, in 2000, it appeared that anywhere from 2,700 to 3,400 languages might benefit from a language development, educational and translation project. In addition, many languages had already received some level of attention. This left 15 percent to 23 percent or 1,000 to 1,500 languages either nearing extinction or endangered in that children were not learning the language from their parents and the language was not being used for most daily activities. So, between one in six and one in four of the world's languages were in trouble. To bring this up to date, the 2016 edition of the Ethnologue states that one third of all languages are now endangered.

Some have suggested that perhaps 90 percent of the world's languages will disappear by the year 2100.[19] Proposals that are more modest suggest 50 percent. In fact, no one really knows what the result of language endangerment will be, but language death is certain for a number of languages. The 2016 Ethnologue[20] currently lists 469 languages as nearly moribund

---

18. Grimes, *Ethnologue*.
19. Krauss, "World's Languages in Crises," 4–10.
20. Krauss, "World's Languages in Crises," 4–10.

or nearly extinct and 220 as dormant or extinct. On the other hand, 53 percent of the currently spoken languages have fewer than 10,000 speakers. Having a smaller population base, however, does not indicate that they are necessarily endangered. Some of these are endangered if they are spoken in the context of a major language. Others may not be since they may be spoken in the context of a number of other languages with less than 10,000 speakers, or they may be relatively isolated from other languages. A major factor in this matter is "language ecology." The region in which a group of languages is spoken is more critical to the health of a given language than the mere statistic of the number of speakers. Measuring language viability and prophesying their long-term demise is a complex issue with various factors interacting in the social environment.

Another issue is the speed at which language recession and extinction might take place. About 500 languages will disappear in this generation unless something dramatic happens. Other languages may not go extinct for another two or three generations. In these cases, the realization that they may go extinct before 2100 is not sufficient grounds for ignoring them. Instead, the speakers of these languages are all human beings in need of favorable policies and services from their governments, from interested development agencies, as well as from social and religious institutions.

One of the crucial measures in responding to requests from communities is that leaders of the language community recognize the need for programs that are relevant to the community's use of their language. A big part of this measure is the degree to which the community itself is willing to participate and contribute to the development of their language. Ultimately the language belongs to the community.

The 2016 Ethnologue[21] includes these additional crucial points: 1) more than half of the world's populations speaks one of only 23 languages, 2) nearly two-thirds of the world's languages are spoken in Africa and Asia, 3) 86 percent of the world's population use an Asian or European language because of the large populations found in those regions, and 4) languages in the Pacific as well as North and South America average 1,000 speakers but they represent more than one-third of the world's languages—among the most disenfranchised populations at the global level, but hold a significant portion of our human linguistic heritage.

---

21. Lewis et al., *Ethnologue*.

Continuing assessment of language viability

Being aware of endangered languages and the potential for languages to disappear in the near future has led some linguists to look more closely at how the health and viability of the languages of the world might be measured. M. Paul Lewis, Gary F. Simons, and D. H. Whalen have developed a scale for assessing the status of language development versus language endangerment.[22] They have elaborated the "Graded Intergenerational Disruption Scale (GIDS)" developed by Fishman.[23] The scale provides a way to measure how likely a given language is to shift from one level of use to another. The scale provides a categorization of languages from those that have the status of an official national language, highest on the scale at level 1, to those that have diminished in use to the point of dying or almost disappeared, the lowest on the scale at level 8. By taking Fishman's scale as well as the UNESCO framework for endangered languages and the *Ethnologue* vitality categories, they have sought to harmonize the three into what they refer to as an "Extended GIDS" or "EGIDS." The results of their harmonization and evaluation are recorded for every language of the world, beginning with the nineteenth edition of the *Ethnologue*.[24]

Lewis and Simons develop a set of five key questions that serve as a decision tree. It provides a transparent means to determine to which category a given language belongs.

Key Question #1:
What is the current identity function of the language?

They propose a four way split in answer to this question, but in another sense there is a major two way split between the extinct (Level 10) and dormant (Level 9) languages on one hand and all the rest on the other. Extinct languages are those that have no one who identifies with it or speaks it, while dormant languages may have a few individuals who identify with the language symbolically even though they are no longer proficient in it. The bulk of the languages of the world fall into the other two categories: vehicular languages and home languages. Vehicular languages are also often

---

22. See Lewis and Simons, "Assessing Endangerment"; Whalen and Simons, "Endangered Language Families"; Simons, "Language Development."

23. See Fishman, *Reversing Language Shift*.

24. Eberhard et al, "Endangered Languages."

referred to as "languages of wider communication (LWCs)" in that there are those who speak them as their first language as well as many others who speak it at varying levels as their second or additional language. Home languages are those spoken only or largely within the community, that has it as their first language.

Key Question #2: What is the level of official use?

This question is relevant to those languages that are "vehicular"—those that are spoken beyond the borders of those who speak it as their first language. The key word in this question is "official." They distinguish three types of official languages: those with an international scope (Level 0), those with a national scope (Level 1), and those with a regional (sub-national—Level 2) scope. The fourth category of vehicular languages (LWCs) is not officially recognized but still have a role beyond their homeland borders. They are referred to as "trade" languages or "languages of wider communication" (Level 3). Many if not most of these languages are developed and in wide use in multiple domains and institutions. This is especially true for the officially recognized languages: international, national and regional. In some cases, the trade languages may still be in need of further attention.

Key Question #3:
Are all parents transmitting the language to their children?

This question is relevant to those languages that are "home" languages. The critical factor here is the intergenerational transmission that may or may not take place. In the case of those languages in which parents are teaching their children the local language, a next question further distinguishes sub-categories:

Key Question #4: What is the literacy status?

In this case, the distinguishing feature is the status of literacy in the home language. It may already be institutionalized in the education system, and so be categorized as "educational" (Level 4). It may be incipient, that is, in the process of being introduced but with most in the language community still not taught to read their language. Such languages would be categorized as "written" or "developing" (Level 5). The third category is languages in which no literacy is taking place (most often because the language has no written form). The language, however, is still used across all generations. These languages are categorized as "vigorous"(Level 6a).

Clearly in the "educational" category, the language is already being taught in educational institutions. However, in the "written" category where literacy is incipient and the "vigorous" category the languages would benefit from attention and efforts by governments, NGOs, churches and others with interest in language use. If the community wants to maintain their language, the assistance of national and international institutions could make a significant difference in sustaining the language as a community value and resource.

Key question #5:
What is the youngest generation of proficient speakers?

The fifth question distinguishes sub-groups of those languages that are left, those that are not vehicular, not official, with no written form, and in which not all children are learning the language from their parents. In the most positive case, where most individuals from all generations are speaking the language, the language would be categorized as "threatened" (Level 6b). However, if the children no longer speak the language but parents and other older generations still speak it, then the language is "shifting" (Level 7). If only the grandparents and great grandparents speak the language, it is "moribund" (Level 8a), and if only the great grandparents are speaking, it is "nearly extinct" (Level 8b). Once the grandparents die, the language will be extinct.

In this group of languages, those that are "threatened" would in particular benefit from efforts to promote language development in the community. This would be especially true if the community is interested and committed to making a difference in the lives of its own members. Once efforts move to the "shifting," "moribund," and "nearly extinct" it will be a struggle to make a difference except for the generation that still speaks the language. For their benefit and well being, if they are interested, specially defined projects could be put in place that meet the communication and knowledge needs of those who still speak the language. These programs would most likely make sense with the "shifting" languages and maybe some "moribund" ones.

It is not envisaged that these programs would involve the same kind of effort and resources needed to support "threatened," "vigorous," and "written" languages.

In order to arrive at a picture of the trend regarding language endangerment over the past 60 years, Lewis and Simons report that languages that were being spoken in 1950 now have the current 2016 status as indicated in Table 6.

Levels	Summary categories	Number of languages	(%) of spoken languages
0, 1, 2, 3, 4	Institutional	572	8
5	Developing	1,619	23
6a	Vigorous	2,462	35
6b, 7	In trouble	1,524	21
8a, 8b, 9	Dying	920	13
10	Extinct	202	

Table 6: Status in 2016 of languages spoken in 1950

The most salient and perhaps the most indicative feature of the direction that a language is moving is the intergenerational one. If parents are teaching their children the language of the community, i.e., the "vigorous" category and above, it is likely that the language will continue to be present in some form for at least the next generation and beyond. If the children are not learning the language of the community, it is possible that in two or three generations the language will have completely fallen into disuse and disappear.

Language endangerment is being accounted for in the identification of the number of languages being spoken and assessment of language vitality is continuing to be evaluated so that those languages that could l benefit from language development are identified. Certainly, those languages in the categories 'threatened' and above should receive attention from the variety of institutions that can engage in assisting them to use their language in various domains. Below that category, special projects may be possible that would assist the remaining speakers of the given language to benefit from its use.

Conclusion

Minority languages are equally among the wonders of human life along with the majority languages. Minority languages are spoken by communities that make up the "bottom billion" or "bottom two billion" people of the earth. Their languages are fully developed expressions of human linguistic innovation and creativity. They deserve respect from those who speak majority languages that dominate the linguistic world. As matters of equity and justice, governments, NGOs, religious organizations such as churches, and others should give them even greater attention and investment of resources. In some cases, the minority communities have some ideas of what is possible and who would benefit from assistance in achieving it. In many cases they still need to be informed as to what could be done to further develop their languages so they can serve the social, cultural, political, economic and spiritual needs and goals of the community of speakers for coming generations. There are tools at our disposal to assess the possibilities for a given language community, so we have little excuse other than the disinterest or resistance from some of the minority communities in further developing their languages. There is no excuse for a lack of socio-political will on the part of the majority language communities and their decision-makers to benefit these communities. This includes government institutions, NGOs, churches and religious organizations. It is possible and should be imperative to include in the development of a given nation the development and use of its minority languages alongside its major languages to the benefit of all its citizens.

4

Independence to Interdependence
The Way to Fulfill the Great Commission in the Twenty-First Century

PAUL R. GUPTA

It was in the early 1970's when Dr. Billy Graham asked the questions "Is it possible by the turn of the century this world can be evangelized for Christ?" and "What must we do to harvest the largest number into the kingdom of God?" It was such thinking that led to the 1974 Lausanne Conference on World Evangelism. Over 2,600 missional leaders from over 150 countries attended this epochal conference. Papers were presented, discussions ensued, and recommended changes were offered, all to envision and mobilize the church towards the vision of discipling all Nations.

In these forty years since Lausanne, I believe there have been five significant strategic changes that resulted in the great harvest the global church has experienced. The first change was that *national churches took responsibility for the Great Commission.* They were encouraged to embrace their birthright and establish new movements. This resulted in missional movements on every continent. A second change was a shift that put greater *focus on unreached people groups,* giving highest priority to those who have never heard the gospel. This resulted in a significant impact among formerly unreached people groups, where suddenly thousands Bible believing, indigenous, reproducing worshiping communities that were newly formed. A third strategic change was *the merging of the great command with the great commission*, enabling the church to offer a more holistic gospel so the marginalized could experience not only a message of hope but also the unconditional love demonstrated by the body of Christ. The fourth significant change was a greater embrace of the practice of *contextualization*, which increased the church's effectiveness in communication and comprehension of the gospel message and enhanced the frequency of indigenous worshiping forms being used in the global Christian community. The final, but most significant change that has transformed the progress of the church toward fulfilling the Great Commission was the realization that the command in the Great Commission was *to make disciples of all nations*. This pivotal move shifted much of the church from a focus on growing by addition to that of multiplication, from simple presence and/or proclamation to creating new worshipping communities. Though precise figures are difficult to collect and verify, it is clear that the result of this important change has an addition of untold millions of new disciples to the global church, with astonishingly large numbers of new churches planted.

For example, Jack Dennison indicates that during the last 40 years the Church in South America has averaged 10,000 people per day that come to Jesus Christ. For Africa, estimates place numbers around 140,000 people that enter the kingdom of God every week. In China, each month a new 900,000 Chinese are added to the Christian family. According to Dennison's research, daily some 165,000 people come to Christ worldwide. He notes that this is an increase from around 70,000 in the beginning of the nineties, up a staggering 100,000 per day by the middle of that decade.

This Global phenomenon of great numerical growth requires us to ask the question "How do we join in what God is doing?" What must we do now in order to harvest the receptive, evangelize the unreached and finish the task in our generation? We must address these age-old questions in each generation, under every socio political transformation so that we can carry out the mission in the most strategic manner as possible. We must step back, evaluate the past, understand the present, and project into the future.

Understanding the Past to Step into the Future: The Era of Modern Missions

Missions as we know it today is the result of the great Reformation when Martin Luther launched his revolution with a focus that Salvation is by faith and faith alone and revelation is from scripture and scripture alone. He created a great revolutionary movement for the church and world missions. But, it was not until William Carrey, the father of modern missions, motivated by this great Reformation change, who asked intentionally the questions about how will the heathen come to know the salvation of our God if they did not hear? Thank God that William Carrey did not listen to the voice of the hyper-Calvinistic theologians, who discouraged human agency and responsibility in the evangelization of the nations. Instead, Carrey chose to go, despite significant discouragement and protestations. It was Carrey who revealed a new paradigm for the mission of the church. This new approach included learning a new language, facilitating the translation of the Scripture, establishing church movements, enabling the transformation of society, establishing educational institutions, and developing communities of believers.

Despite the deserved criticism leveled against early Protestant missionaries for developing the mission compound strategy and lacking the sensitivity and vision to develop national leadership, God was still. Through their imperfect efforts, God established His church all around the world, making the Christian community a truly global phenomenon for the first time in history.

A great tragedy of this period was demonstrated in the Western mission leaders' inability to read and respond appropriately to the handwriting on the wall. As early as 1910, mission leaders at the Edinburgh Conference were convinced that the era of the great European Colonial powers would end. There was a cry for the development of national leadership. However, they did not see or understand the impact of neglecting to develop adequate leadership for this vital transition. By 1950, national movements in various parts of the world began to reject missionary entry. Eventually, many countries would expel expatriate missionaries. At times this rejection of foreign influence was painfully stated in the slogan "Missionary, go home."

Missions in the period of Nationalization

In 1974, Dr. Billy Graham, the convener of the Lausanne Conference, spoke to attendees. Looking across the gathering, he expressed great disappointment in how the church had been unable to see the growing ability of national leadership. Nationalization had started and was now at its peak. Yet a full 85 percent of conference attendees were still expatriates. Dr. Graham strongly addressed the issue and directly charged the expatriates to go back and turn leadership over to national leaders. He implored the national leaders to exercise their birthright and establish new church movements, mission agencies and parachurch organizations that represented indigenous identity.

During this period of renewed nationalization, mission efforts by national churches experienced a slow beginning. Yet, within ten years following the 1974 Lausanne Conference, churches began to see unprecedented growth. All over the world churches began to grow. Strong national indigenous church movements and local leadership began to emerge. Dennison notes that between the 1960 and 1985 the Church worldwide experienced an annual average growth rate of 1 percent—not even keeping with the rate of global population increase. Yet, from 1985–1990 a sharp acceleration began which resulted in a growth rate of 3 percent. During the first five years of the 1990s this growth rate had increased to 5 percent, and during the subsequent five years 7 percent to 8 percent.

This observation should teach us a very significant lesson in understanding the task of fulfilling the Great Commission. It is that we must not fail to see the handwriting on the wall. We must understand that each generation will experience change. When the socio-political and economic context changes, we need to seek God and see how God wants us to fulfill His mission.

Missions in the context of Globalization

"The walls came down and windows went up" is how Thomas Friedman describes the phenomenon of Globalization in his book "The World is Flat."[1] Unfortunately, as was the case in the early twentieth century, very few movements or church leaders saw the potential and opportunities to develop a new paradigm in the context of the new era we now term

---

1. Friedman, "World is Flat," 50.

Globalization. The mission societies and denominational movements saw opportunities but failed to learn from the past and fell into what Dr. Sherwood Lingenfelter called a "default mode." That is, we sent missionaries the same old way without stepping back and asking what would be the best way to capitalize on the unique opportunities in this new era.

If Globalization teaches us anything, it is that we exist in a context of interdependence and we must work against the tendency to do things independently. When Christians work together, such interdependency results in greater empowerment. We must learn to bring together our resources, people, information and ideas and unite them in a synergetic environment so that we can become God's most powerful instruments to fulfill the mission of Jesus Christ.

Understanding Interdependency

In his book *The 7 Habits of Highly Effective People*, Steven Covey develops the idea that all people go through different stages of relationality. He begins by noting how a child is born in dependence. The child cannot do anything for itself; the child is dependent on the parent. Yet a time comes when the child learns from observation and personal growth and becomes more and more independent. Eventually, children move out and go "on their own." Covey says most people get to this stage and think, "I finally made it," yet fail to see that there is another stage—interdependence. Interdependence is a state where we recognize the power and ability of others and allow our weakness to be supplemented by the strengths of others, creating a context of synergy and trust (viz., interdependency) to accomplish greater things than we could do by our own independent efforts.

Biblical Understanding of Interdependence

The Apostle Paul said, we are one Body and Christ is the Head of the Body. We have one God, one Spirit, one Hope, one Lord and One faith (Eph 4:4–6). God desires oneness similar to that of the Godhead. This is an organic oneness, not a collection of independent parts. Jesus prayed Father let them be one even as we are one (John 17:21). God does not encourage the concept of working independently or in isolation. If we are to accomplish the task of the Master, we must recognize that Christ is our Head, and we are all interdependent members of the one Body of Christ. We have to work in oneness that is organic. We must complement and supplement our efforts in fulfilling the desire of the Head, who is Christ.

God designed the church to be a community that functions best in the context of interdependence. When we understand interdependence and the Headship of Jesus Christ we see each part of the body as both complementing and supplementing. This is the way that interdependence can become possible.

Globalization and Interdependence

Many have looked upon Globalization with great fear, as a threat that portends a one-world global economy. In a similar way, the church has shied away from the potential opportunities Globalization offers. Have we blinded ourselves by a fear of Globalization from seeing how this new globalizing era could enable the Church to further the commission Christ gave to the church?

In the colonial context, God used the West to lay a foundation for a truly global church. These early workers labored in independence because there were no indigenous partners with whom they could build partnerships. During the subsequent stage of nationalization, while the doors were closing for many, nationals worked in independence and God taught them to rise up and learn how to serve the mission of the church in their own national contexts. Now, in the globalizing era, the church and mission societies must shift to interdependence, building healthy relationality and developing significant partnerships.

Many mission societies and organizations still send missionaries independently. Some of these go on student visas, others on tourist visas, some with business visas. Unfortunately, much of this still occurs independently of the national church movements.

Notable exceptions to this independent approach are organizations that partner with nationals on short-term mission projects. Agencies such as Wycliffe saw the value of interdependent partnerships and made a major paradigm shift and joined hands with national movements, blending their capacities to accelerate the process of fulfilling the mission. Networking movements like Mission One saw clearly the value of bringing the nationals and the global church to serve a common vision and build partnerships for fulfilling the vision of God.

Devoted to Christ

I believe what God is seeking to do in this era of Globalization is for the first time in human history to network His body globally to function interdependently. Missions in this era truly has no boundaries. Mission can now literally be from anywhere to everywhere. This includes not only places where God is opening new doors but also the move of God's church to the nations from the east to the west. He is moving the unreached from every corner of the globe and bringing the mission field to our doorsteps. Cities that were once primarily mono-cultural are now becoming increasingly multi-cultural and pluralistic. We should ask the question, what does this mean to us? Why is God doing this?

An example of this is how the Chinese government is asking many Chinese professors to spend a year in research at a US university. Some Chinese Christians are meeting them and discipling them and introducing them to the Lord. What if Churches worked with the Chinese Christians and created interdependent partnerships so our churches are blessed to invest in the new believers who will be with us for a year and go back and be part of relationships in their own country?

In the last 40 years, despite our inability to see what God was doing and appropriately respond to Him, He established mission movements and enabled mission from every continent. At one time, mission was from the West to the rest. This has changed. For example, Korea is now one of the largest mission-sending nations of the world. Believers in Singapore are not only supporting and sending missionaries but have also began to facilitate large numbers of short-term missions. India is quickly becoming one of the largest senders of cross-cultural missionaries (such includes those sent both inside and outside the sub-continent). Christians in China are talking about taking the journey "back to Jerusalem." South America is sending missionaries to the Middle East and other parts of the world. Filipino churches are sending tent makers and serving the Lord as a voice in the wilderness. We have many missions sending nations all over the world. What does this mean for the Church? What opportunities does such provide for interdependence?

Missions over the past 20 years have produced incredible results. For the first time in the history of the modern church, more than 65 percent of the church is non-white with a large part of the church existing in the Global south. The church has truly become global and mission is now truly mission without boundaries.

The global economy is moving from the west to Asia. Once nations that were dependent are now able to move from dependency to interdependency. Once nations that were so independent, isolated, and self-sustained under nationalization, have become interdependent. How does this lend itself to interdependence in missions?

Globalization has changed the face of the world and the operating system can no longer be the same. Things have changed and missions need to ask the question of what needs to be the paradigm in today's context.

A New Paradigm of Interdependence

Certainly the day of sending missionaries through mission societies to do mission as it was done in the era of colonization is the thing of the past. The weaknesses inherent in the paradigm of nationals independently working to reach their own nation are clear now. We must now consider seriously a new paradigm of interdependence. Locally, Churches, parachurch organizations, and mission societies must ask how they can work together and disciple those coming to their door steps and find the most effective ways to harness the global church to interdependently serve one another.

It is very easy for ethnic communities from different parts of the world to gather independently, creating local homogeneous communities of Christ. Tamil Christians coming to Chicago may find themselves gathering with Tamil Christians from India because the local churches have not given opportunities to embrace them and utilize their skills, abilities and giftedness. Local churches should recognize how God is bringing not only the unevangelized world into their context but also gifted people to help local churches reach out to the unreached that are at their door steps. In a context of interdependence, the larger body of Christ needs to be empowered to enable the opportunities God is bringing into our context. With such interdependent partnerships, believing Tamils can reach unbelieving Tamils.

Missions is from anywhere to everywhere and from everywhere to anywhere. As people from all over the world are coming to our contexts, we need to learn to become interdependent and allow Christ to lead His body to reach out and enable them to jointly serve in discipling a pluralistic world in which we are living. Churches will soon become multicultural as we increase our interdependency and allow God to work through His manifold giftedness in the body of Christ.

Devoted to Christ

How can we create such interdependence through the process of building partnership? How do we facilitate changes to maximize these opportunities? The paradigm of partnership building does have the capacity of moving the church to interdependence but there is a great deal of newness to it and therefore there exists a great need to understand clearly the process of developing such partnerships.

What is Partnership?

The term partnership originally gained popularity in the secular world when independent proprietorships realized that the demand for their products was greater than their ability to produce them. Because of their difficulty of limited resources, they invited partners who invested in a joint enterprise, shared profits, helped meet demands, and accomplished their vision.

Today the Church is in a similar situation. The task of completing the Great Commission is enormous, complex and the harvest is beyond expectation for any one organization to complete with its limited resources or in independence. The Church-at-large must realize the need and potential of jointly participate in completing the task. Developing such partnerships will help global churches develop strategic programs to fulfill the great commission locally and globally—programs that can complement and supplement the resources of the larger Body of Christ in a synergetic context to enable it to disciple the nations to Christ.

Toward a Working Definition On Partnership

How then should we define Partnership? The Indian Partnership Act, which regulates partnership business in India defines partnership as "the relationship between persons who have agreed to share the profit of a business carried on by all or any of them acting for all."[2]

Bush and Lutz in their book on partnering in ministry define partnership as "an association of two or more autonomous bodies who have formed a trusting relationship and fulfill an agreed upon expectation by sharing complementary strengths and resources, to reach their mutual goal."[3]

---

2. "Indian Partnership Act," §44(d).
3. Bush and Lutz, *Partnering in Ministry*, 46.

Edelman, Carr, and Lancaster suggest that partnership is a "voluntary organized process by which multiple stakeholders having shared interests perform as a team to achieve mutually beneficial goals . . . building trusting relationships, and engaging in collaborative problem solving."[4]

Each of these definitions highlights important elements that form what I consider the ingredients for a comprehensive notion of partnership. Here I wish to identify and augment several ingredients that lead to what in my mind constitute healthy and functional forms of functional partnerships.

Key Elements of a healthy Missional Partnership.

1. Two or more persons or institutions must come together to form a mutually beneficial and interdependent working relationship.
2. A common vision that elaborates how partners believe God is calling them to accomplish and mutually develop goals, values, objectives, plans and strategies to accomplish the project.
3. All partners jointly invest resources for the benefit of all.
4. Partners mush work toward building a synergistic environment to carry out the project at a higher level of effectiveness.
5. A clear contract must exist that lays out the involvements, investments, expectations and anticipation of each party is part of every partnership.
6. This contract must include a method of evaluation that generates periodic reports to ensure the plan is proceeding as projected.
7. Christ is the head of this partnership.

For the purpose of the mission of the church, I believe it is critical to understand how partnerships as a working relationship between Christ and parts of His body can come together, locally or globally, to accomplish great things. They share a common purpose and values to fulfill a common vision God has placed in their heart. Partners prayerfully develop mutually agreed upon goals, objectives, plans and strategies and agree to bring investors and investments to a projected budget. They facilitate a synergistic environment of transparency by working together, reporting and evaluating the progress of the mission until the completion of the project.

4. Edelman et al., *Partnering*, 2.

Devoted to Christ

All over the world individuals and institutions are entering into these types of partnerships. The time is right for such people to work together to achieve common goals. We are living in a period when one cannot work independently of the other's activities, especially in relation to those who work is similar to that of their mission. When the world is moving into a state of interdependency and internationalization, we as a Church need to also demonstrate our oneness in building Christ's kingdom.

As we work towards discipling nations for Christ, the ecclesia, the mission societies and parachurch organizations must see the need for each other, the power in working in partnerships and come to some working system so we can harvest the unreached and fulfill the vision of incarnating the glory of God to cover the earth as the water covers the sea.

How do we build partnership?

Interdependence does not happen automatically. It is fraught with pitfalls and dangers. As a national Christian leader trained in the West, I would like to share several principles from my perspective that I believe are crucial for effective partnerships.

We must mutually agree that the partnership be purpose driven, motivated by vision, sustained by values, and implemented by strategic plans. Too often partnerships are developed with a little or no attempt to synchronize purpose, articulate vision and establish values. Without these, it is difficult to accomplish the objectives of a partnership.

Every partner must bring resources to the table. If all parties do not bring resources, the relationship is not partnership. Inequality in controlling resources leads to ownership. Such will lead to controlling dynamics from the side of the owner. Partnerships must inevitably develop intentional patterns where all parties state their purpose for coming together, the vision they would like to accomplish, and the strategy they would like to employ. But, after they have developed the vision and strategy together they must determine the total resources needed to accomplish the combined objectives of the partnership, and clearly decide who is bringing what to the table. It is critical to the partnership to not begin with the resources. First, give yourselves time to understand what God is calling you to do. Then, and only then, and then worry about resources.

In order for a partnership to develop and prosper, each participant should clearly state what kind of resources and in what proportion each would bring into the partnership. By doing so, it will be clear from the beginning that there is joint ownership for this task and the resources are shared resources. Establishing clear understandings of resource contributions and sharing ahead of time will help prevent finances or other resources from controlling the partnership.

In addition, it is essential to remember that *all resources* belong to God. We are merely stewards and are dependent on Him for everything. Regardless of who provides the finances and what proportions each person brings to the partnership, all must be considered as coming from God, not merely from a human partner. By doing so, we will guard against letting resources control the partnership.

We must build trust in order to develop effective partnerships. It takes time to build trust in any human relationship. So too in ministry partnerships it will take time for both parties to truly develop a context in which they mutually trust each other unconditionally. This is especially important when a partnership involves the added complication that cross-cultural or multi-cultural relationships inherently bring.

Churches and ministries need to create environments that will create this kind of trust. We must not have partnerships that are all money and no involvement. We all have people resources in our churches and mission societies that could be great assets to the partnership. We must bring all of this into the mix when we are building relationships and understanding our partners. If we are to build partnerships on mutual trust, there must be genuine relationship and interaction on the project. Where relationship is lacking there will be little or no trust established in the partnership. It is only when we develop significant trust that we can be truly accountable to each other.

We must create clearly defined goals. Too often a mission project is supported with no defined beginning or end. For years churches have invested resources not knowing exactly what they will accomplish. As a result, nothing significant is ultimately achieved. We all must learn to identify the task and work towards the completion of the project.

Especially when there are more than two entities in a partnership, it is essential for building the partnership to have a clear vision with clear expectations, and an agreed-upon methodology that partners can us to properly evaluate work and progress. This way, every one in the partnership understands and visualizes the progress that is being made.

Yet, because we are weak human vessels, partnerships are complicated even more by the challenges of cross-cultural dynamics. Since this is so, we must work hard to build into the system a process that facilitates reconciliation when communication breaks down, or when failure is experienced in the vision or values of the partnership. This will enable the partnership to remain focused on its tasks and move effectively towards the clearly defined goals it has established together.

We must be prepared to make adjustments. Partnerships are like a marriage. The husband and wife must learn to make adjustments and develop a way to make the marriage work. In every partnership there is an adjustment period; there are bugs in the system that need to be cleaned out. As partners begin the relationship, they learn the meaning of these expectations and understand the limitations that cause delays.

In most cases, these partnerships will involve working cross-culturally. Therefore we should expect challenges. Because it is not just a marriage but also a cross-cultural marriage, most partnerships will require greater-than-normal adjustments. We must not practice "divorce" but do as Jesus would do, that is, bring reconciliation and understanding to the relationship until it deepens and becomes more effective.

When expectations are unclear and communication breaks down, partnerships experience trauma. The church must understand that in working with multicultural relationships, much in a partnership will not go smoothly. When such partnership relational bumps do occur, the church's first response should be to genuinely seek to interact with the partner before grabbing for the jugular vein.

We must have a written agreement. This agreement should spell out clearly the steps and expectations are spelled out. It should be written jointly so that both parties are a full part, and so prevent misunderstandings regarding the vision, values and objectives of the partnership. This process must make provision for each partner to read the document, raise questions for understanding, change the wording where necessary, and finally sign. The agreement should clearly state the beginning and end time to fulfill the purpose, vision and objectives of the partnership.

Too often partners leave agreements in oral form. Often, however, the specifics of such oral agreements are forgotten, redefined (without mutual consent), or misunderstood. Especially when working in the context of cross-cultural realities, it is very important to document everything. In preparing the agreement jointly there is opportunity for clarification, reduction of misunderstanding, and clear legitimization. Above all, a written agreement provides a document for reference, should things become difficult and jeopardize the completion of the objectives of the partnership.

Finally, *we develop partnerships with the objective to finish the Great Commission.* Often, partnerships fail to begin with the end in mind and miss the importance of finishing the task, letting other more proximate goals divert partner attention from this most important, overarching goal for every Christian partnership. I believe if the church is going to contribute effectively to the fulfillment of the Great Commission and build strategic partnerships, the church must educate itself thoroughly about the completion of the task. It must ask itself the question, "How can we effectively contribute so that we can build partnerships that will result in finishing the Great Commission?"

Whether it is by contributing to the development of indigenous leadership—or by the mobilization of a church planting movement among an unreached people group—it is important that in building partnerships, all parties must ask the question, "How are we helping to finish the task?"

Conclusion

In closing, I believe the path is to overcome current challenges and the way to greatest change is to equip the local church and seek to understand what God is doing today in our context. We must resist the temptation of falling back into our default modes. We must seek to educate mission committees in local churches of the new day we are to help them understand the new opportunities and enable them to build new paradigms that will enable the process of facilitating interdependency in the context of a new day in fulfilling the mission of God.

We must equip the church to understand it exists to build God's kingdom. We are the body and He is the head. We are all His instruments and we must learn to listen to God, identifying partners with similar vision and values, and build partnerships to fulfill God's mission. We must allow Him to lead the way and transform our lives, communities and societies through the process of being reconciled to God. We are in the process of discipling our constituents to trust Him and allow the working of His Holy Spirit in their lives.

We need to train the church to understand what it *can do* and *cannot do* in a partnership. We must resist the temptation of giving the church the opinion it is possible to plant a church in five days through a short-term mission trip. We should equip them to understand that they are a step toward completing the process. Wrong expectations can result in loss of faith and we may loose partnerships if partners have unrealistic expectations.

Additionally, it is important to train churches to understand that sometimes all they should do is pray, work with small groups, and engage in development work. Then they will not get their expectations higher than they should be, thinking *they* will be planting churches.

Missions is not the agenda of any one nation nor is it primarily a Western enterprise. It is the task of the global church and there are no geographical or national boundaries. Every church movement in the world is ready to carry out the Great Commission. We must ask ourselves "How can we partner with these movements so that the greatest effectiveness can be achieved through our joint effort in fulfilling the mission of God?"

We can make a huge difference in fulfilling the great commission in our generation. We must recognize what God is doing today and align ourselves with His agenda and be willing to make the necessary changes absolutely trusting Him. We must become a church that is interdependent and partner with each other, keeping in mind the end goal under the Lordship of Jesus Christ. Let's work together! This is what true partnership represents.

5

Navigating Power
Liquid Power Structures for Molten Times

ANITA KOESHALL

The little church (henceforth referred to as Church B) now was located in an economically depressed neighborhood. At one time, the flourishing industry in the city had been the backdrop of a large active church. The pastor, although authoritarian, was loved and highly respected. Together, the people of Church B opened a coffee house that attracted youth off the street. The pastor could often be found at a table, coffee in hand, in intense conversation with these teens.

That was now all past. The pastor had moved on to a national church office. Several church elders had assumed positions of power, and pastors that followed tangled with them only so long before moving on to more promising places of ministry. Membership dwindled, seemingly in correspondence to the economic downturn. The church managed to break the power of the original elders in a turbulent business meeting, and a younger man and his wife became the sole church elders. This young man instituted an egalitarian "democratic" church structure, fiercely protecting the little church from hierarchical leadership, which was a relief after decades of power abuse. Now most members were pleased with the opportunity to discuss important church issues, but some remained unconvinced that this new egalitarian structure was "biblical."

Devoted to Christ

A leader's task is to guide the flow of relational power within the community of faith through turbulent social, generational, and demographic shifts in its outer environment and the dynamics of change internally. More than simply creating job descriptions and assigning roles, leadership involves the process of bringing people to maturity; that is, enabling members to be reflexive agents who think biblically, exegete their culture, and envision the mission that God has for them.

These actions—determining truth, defining vision, analyzing cultural situations, and assigning resources to fulfill vision—belong to the domain of power. Leaders who exercise and distribute power in a redeemed manner recognize the gifts of members and give them space to serve, bringing members to maturity and enthusiastic participation in the organization.

I wish to deal with two formative elements for the task of navigating power in liquid times: culture change and a biblical understanding of power employed in church structures. First, I highlight two churches (Church B and Church C) that will serve to demonstrate how relational power patterns from the wider culture play a significant role in what is deemed legitimate in the church itself. Such a tendency to assimilate the structural ideals of the default culture, if unconscious, may be detrimental to the life of a church even though the structures are legitimized by the greater society. Second, I propose a biblical understanding of power that may serve as an anchor in the complex process of transforming structures for relevant ministry in changing times and demographics. Christian organizations often fail to develop a biblical understanding of power, to articulate it often, and allow it to critique and correct their organization. When ignored or feared, power takes on a life of its own and can corrupt even those who hold the best of intentions.

The Enigma of Power

The abuse of power has befuddled the church throughout the centuries. The distribution of power lies at the heart of any human social organization and shapes all interactions and relationships. Anthropologist Mary Douglas offers a way to chart power distribution in an organization, using a dimension she terms grid.

On the high end of grid, a hierarchy tends to monopolize positions of prominence, control privilege, and perpetuate the dominant ideology through insulation and centralization. At the low end of Grid, an egalitarian organization atomizes power and allows individuals to choose whom they will follow—if anyone—and to interpret truth themselves.

Hierarchies, with their propensity to extend themselves geographically and generationally, have proven historically that, when in evil hands, they possess great capacity for abusing power and creating havoc in families, organizations, and nations. At the low end of the Grid, where power is atomized rather than centralized, participants within egalitarian organizations experience difficulty pinpointing the foci of power. The resulting "leaderless" social structure potentially drives manipulation, politicking, and competition for control underground. Power plays frequently generate destructive divisions; egalitarians have limited capacity to unite a large number of citizens to accomplish good.

Regardless of the structure, power is infamous for both the abuses that have come from high-grid tyrannical leaders and low-grid manipulative members. Everyone, it seems, wants to exercise power but regards with suspicion those who do so.

When power has been abused, a frequent solution is to redistribute power, usually changing from a hierarchy to an egalitarian structure, as seen in Church B.

This reshuffling of structure neither eliminates the trap of power nor answers the concern that resonates particularly in churches and organizations that desire to escape it. It sidesteps the basic question of how leadership can be practiced without employing power.

Church B belongs to the Pentecostal Churches in Germany, which broke away from the hierarchical structures of the German State Church at the beginning of the twentieth century, but then resorted to the default culture of the early twentieth century German society.

More recently the Emerging Church movement is, among other things, a testimony to the desire to reframe power contrary to the standards of modernity. Spokesmen from that movement complain,

> Their [the modern churches'] leadership is based on power, control and submission to authority. For the church to resemble the kingdom of God, current notions of church power must be drastically altered. The church needs to operate as a consensual process in which all have a say in influencing outcomes.[1]

---

1. Gibbs and Bolger, *Emerging Church*, 192.

Members of this movement have opted to reorient power distribution from hierarchy to egalitarianism, as Eddie Gibbs and Ryan Bolger recorded: "In a nonhierarchical community, all members help make decisions and take turns leading, actions that serve as a counter to the control and oppressive tendencies of modernity."[2]

In such an egalitarian setting, power may appear non-operative, or at least not susceptible to evil ends; however, even egalitarian organizations find that ill-defined power can become manipulative and disenchanting.

The Scriptures give neither hierarchical nor egalitarian organization primacy.

A faith community must organize so that the community fulfills its mission to image the Triune God and extend God's grace in its own particular context. Patterns of power must remain fluid for changing circumstances. Leaders must move with wisdom and courage to shed an old form of organization and discover other ways to structure with changing times and growing members. Often the Spirit serves as the driving force that pushes communities out of their comfort zones and presses them to experiment with unexplored ecclesiologies and power structures.

Molten Culture and Concretized Church Structures

The leadership of Church B failed to guide the church through the process of biblically critiquing its own power structures. Instead, the church, perhaps unconsciously, assumed the power practices current in secular society. Church B began its life shortly after WWII in a hierarchical cultural context when strong male leadership was the norm. The early pastors, strong, authoritarian, charismatic men, were considered the patriarchs, the shepherds of the flock, the divinely appointed leaders. Following the hierarchical norm, power was centralized in the pastor's hands, with few daring to touch "God's anointed." Pastors were insulated from criticism and were allowed to lead authoritatively. One member reported that even the church architecture reminded the worshippers of their duty to respect spiritual authority; the pastor preached from a raised platform while parishioners gazed upwards to listen. The first pastor, following the turbulent years of WWII, served as a faithful shepherd. The members trusted and followed him gladly as he gathered the discouraged band of believers who had little hope or vision for the future after the war's desolation of their society. A

2. Gibbs and Bolger, *Emerging Church*, 194.

benevolent dictator, the pastor decided truth and determined vision, and the members obediently fulfilled the pastor's vision. But upon the pastor's departure, members were adrift and chaos reigned because the people had not been brought to maturity: they had not helped to define the mission of the community, and they had never shared the responsibility of those decisions. The pastor had led the people adequately for the present but had not prepared them for the future when he would depart and culture would change.

Culture Liquefied

From the 1960s to the 1980s, students took to the streets and began questioning traditional authority structures. The Vietnam War sparked heated controversy, sexual freedom shocked proper citizens, and students insisted on the right to think and act critically, no longer content to simply receive "the truth" from a professor without questioning its validity.

This effected a fundamental change in the values, traditions, and patterns of social interaction. Heated argument aimed to discover truth and was not perceived as an attack on a person. Individualization generated a systematic dis-embedding of individuals from cultural forms, institutions, and traditions without re-embedding.

One's place in society no longer depended on class or family (authoritarian aristocracy), but on skill and ambition (egalitarian meritocracy).

During these years, Church B floundered. The youth (20–40 year olds) of the church sought participation in leadership, open discussion of theology, new modes of worship, and freedom to experiment with church structure. The leadership of Church B, a series of new pastors with a group of aging elders, reacted by becoming more authoritarian.

Feeling attacked when their leadership was questioned, they advocated the stance that the pastor has the vision and the truth and the members were to follow. The difficult upheavals and loss of membership testified to the resulting conflict, leaving the leadership of Church B in the hands of a long time member. This elder felt that the solution to the problem was to make the church as "democratic as possible," corresponding to the present day cultural context.

Going from a hierarchical authoritarian leadership to a democratic, egalitarian structure, however, has not produced life in Church B. On the one hand, the authoritarian pastors of the past expected blind obedience, and indeed had taught that this was biblical. On the other hand, the present elder imposed a democratic social organization without first allowing members the opportunity to examine the Scriptures to critique human power structures. So the present members of Church B find themselves uncomfortable in their own egalitarian skin. They harbor nagging doubts as to whether democratic pursuits are biblically sound, even as they fear pastoral authority because of their history with power abuse. These unhealthy power relationships speak death rather than life to those passing by on the street. The tension with the current culture's egalitarian underpinnings tarnishes the testimony of the church.

Church structures can rightly mimic the culturally accepted hierarchy or egalitarian society, if they serve the church's mission well. But often, the church must defy a cultural pattern to demonstrate a redeemed counter culture. Structures, a social necessity, can empower or enslave. What makes a structure (either hierarchy or egalitarian) empowering in one time and place but enslaving in another? The answer lays in power itself, and how both leader and follower interact with it.

Power to Navigate: A Good Gift Corrupted—and Redeemed

Every community of faith must articulate a theology of power that will serve as a central component of their identity. It begins with acknowledging that God is omnipotent; people are not. This was God's plan for humanity. At creation, God entrusted humans with the power to make decisions (to eat or not to eat of the tree of knowledge of good and evil), the ability to make a difference in their environments, and to act "otherwise" or outside of a pre-determined pattern.

Delegated power to rule over the earth and all that was created was part of their domain. This directive was to be accomplished in relationship, for it was not good that man was alone. The overlap of this call to exercise power with the profoundly relational nature of human existence has for all of human history, produced fundamental human struggle, that is, the sharing power.

The image of God (Gen 1:27), self-expressed in Trinitarian relationships, serves as the plumb line for humanity when they seek to understand relational power in community. God, as Father, Son, and Spirit, revealed in the Scriptures (Gen 1–2; Isa 40:26, 29; Jer 10:12; Col 1:15–20; Heb 1:1–3), is all-powerful, by all sociological definitions of power. He has full capacity to make a difference, to act otherwise;

He created and controls all resources.

Through the Holy Spirit, He has unlimited "networking" capacity;

He defines and embodies all truth and is the author of the operative Narrative.

He is the only one who can claim high power distance—being of a higher essence, living according to a higher rule.

He has charismatic power and legitimate power,

but He refuses to use His power in a Machiavellian way.

As an all-powerful God, there is no need for power striving or hoarding.

God, who is trustworthy and responsible, invests power "otherwise," contrary to the self-protecting, self-aggrandizing, and self-serving human tendencies. In Christ, God demonstrated that the appropriate use of relational power is to serve and expend self for others, as Jesus clearly stated: "The Son of Man came not to be served but to serve, and to give his life as a ransom for many" (Matt 20:28). God demonstrated a particular concern for the poor, the oppressed, the downtrodden, the widow, the orphan, and the alien—people who are disadvantaged by the power holders in the world (Deut 15:11, Ps 82:2–4, Isa 58:7–10; Luke 6:20). He poured himself out, embraced suffering by going to the cross; He became the perfect sacrifice and the great high priest by offering Himself and becoming the servant of all.

> eing in very nature God, [he] did not consider equality with God something to be grasped, but made himself nothing, taking the very nature of a servant, being made in human likeness. And being found in appearance as a man, he humbled himself and became obedient to death—even death on a cross! (Phil 2:6–8)

In a perfect world, all human beings would employ power in the manner that God does, "imaging" His nature as power-givers in society. However, the narrative of Genesis 3 reveals that the desire to dominate was born and has been reified through the generations in forms of physical (and material) strength, patriarchy, the hierarchy-egalitarian dialectic, leadership strivings, and gender clashes. In the arenas in which humankind transacts life, social organization became a necessity because of impending chaos caused by fallen characteristics:

- Plurality of truths—Every human society lacks a grand narrative whereby individuals, nations, and races agree upon an understanding of good and evil; someone must define truth for a community.
- Competing interest groups—Territorialism, manipulation, and control characterize the attitudes and goals of brothers, clans, organizations, and nations.
- Zero-sum power games—Finite, desired resources (be it power, gold, land, prestige, etc.) provoke contests whereby person B can gain only if person A loses.
- Divided wills—Differing desires exist, not only influenced by the material world, but also by the spirit world.
- Broken trust—Self-interest and power-keeping effect non-sustainable relationships, damaging to the grantor and receiver alike.
- Need for self-protection—Protection is purchased with loyalty, walls are built, information withheld, and contracts signed in the face of corruption, uncertain circumstances, and an unknown future.
- Myth of equality—If it were possible to distribute to every person by some technique, the same beginning goods (i.e., education, finances, opportunities), classes and differentiations would continue to exist.

As a result, every culture in the world has developed some mode of social control that is legitimized and incorporated as part of their socialization process.

In fact, humans have *no rational way of conceptualizing or living out life together without social dimensions such as hierarchy and egalitarianism.* As the sociologist Geert Hofstede observed: "The human species belongs to the category that shows dominance behavior. Human pecking orders are part of the 'universal' level of human mental programming."[3]

The church exists in this very human context! God is not uninterested in humanity's attempts to self-organize. He liberated a group of ragtag slaves from the oppressive rule of the Egyptians, He gave them the Law and the Covenant through Moses, and He called them "my people." Judges, prophets, and kings came and went as God patiently persuaded, disciplined, and guided His people to choose to remain faithful to the covenant. Finally, the agony of the incarnational process wrenched Jesus from transcendent glory to embed Him inside human relational structures. His earthly identity was

3. Hoftstede, *Culture's Consequences*, 80.

framed by the social relationships of first century Middle Eastern culture: a Jew under Roman domination, the oldest (albeit seen as an "illegitimate") son of a carpenter, most probably lacking in formal education (Luke 2:41–52), and with little social capital in relationship to the religious ruling class. A subversive, but non-power-seeking leader, He was an unusual rabbi leading a band of followers toward Jerusalem and self-sacrifice. He was a thorn in the sides of the priests, Sadducees, and Pharisees, and trouble for Pilate, the Roman governor.

Christ was confronted with the same power temptations that beset all humanity (Luke 4:1–13), but chose to use His power in a redeemed way, totally counter-rational to human power theories that involve self-protection, self-promotion, and the accumulation of power (cf. Matt 28:18). All-powerful though He was, He invested His rights and privileges, His riches and glory, His control of nature and humanity for the sake of the redemption of the world. The call to His followers consists of a life where the power that one possesses is to be expended that others can live. *Employing power in a redeemed way is a true measure of the transformation of the heart and the submission of the will to Christ, whether by an individual or an organization.*

The church exists in this tension: as an earthly community, the church must structure, organize, and control; as a spiritual community, she is created to follow Christ, mirror His character, and live for the sake of the world.

Power-Striving versus Power-Giving

Geert Hofstede, a Dutch sociologist, added another lens through which power can be explored, reifying the distinction between redeemed and unredeemed power. He defines power as the ability to influence or control another person, and Power Distance (PD) as the "difference between the extent to which B [boss] can determine the behavior of S [subordinate] and the extent to which S can determine the behavior of B."[4]

Mary Douglas's Grid dimension is easily confused with Power Distance; however PD does not necessarily deal with the complexity of an organization, or whether a structure is hierarchical or egalitarian, simply that a subordinate and superior relationship exists. Low Power Distance understands all people to be interdependent, of the same essence, living by rules and expectations that apply equally to all. Leaders play down differences

---

4. Hoftstede, *Culture's Consequences*, 83.

and share rewards with followers. High Power Distance organizations, by contrast, consider leaders to be existentially better, exempt from rules and sanctions, and deserving of special privileges.

Hofstede derives his theories from Mauk Mulder, whose insights into *power striving* are key to this discussion. According to Mulder's hypotheses, the rational dynamics of power in relationships create a system whereby each member of the leader-follower dyad exhibits power-compiling tendencies, as follows:

- The mere exercise of power will give satisfaction.
- The more powerful individual will *strive* to maintain or to increase the power distance to the less powerful person.
- Less powerful individuals will *strive* to reduce the power distance between themselves and more powerful persons.
- The "downward" tendencies of the powerful to *maintain* the power distance and the "upward" power distance reduction of the less powerful *reinforce* each other" (emphasis added; see Figure 1).[5]

Hofstede concludes with the devastating indictment: "Power striving is not fed by dissatisfaction but by satisfaction. Having power feeds the need, making it comparable to the need for hard drugs."[6]

Fortified structures serve to secure the position and prestige of some to the disadvantage of others at the expense of the successful fulfillment of the mission of a community.

---

5. Hoftstede, *Culture's Consequences*, 83.
6. Hoftstede, *Culture's Consequences*, 83.

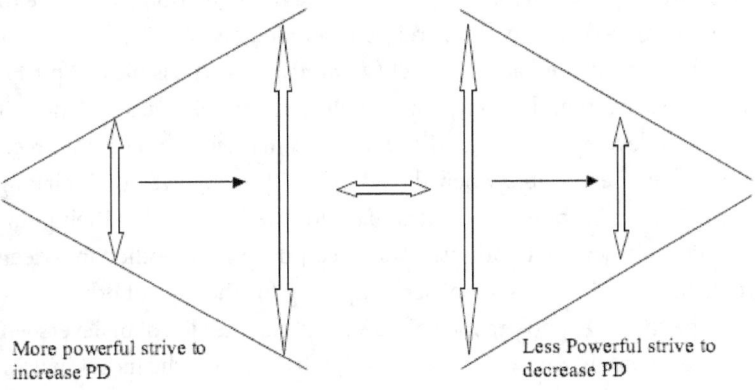

Figure 1. Equilibrium of Power-Striving Tendencies in a Social Environment.

The question of striving for power defines the point of divergence between rational, unredeemed and counter-rational, redeemed power. Power-keeping, lust for power, and zero-sum power games have no legitimate place in a community of faith. When God's Spirit transforms a person, power-striving becomes instead power-giving, a desire to increase the capacity and capabilities of others so that they can best accomplish their part in the mission of the community.

Contrary to the deleterious effects of power-striving, health flows into a community with dynamic relationships between leaders and mature followers in reciprocal service to one another—balanced in asymmetrical tension, as first one leads and then another, depending on the gifts given by the Spirit. In order to navigate power well, individuals with leadership roles of responsibility and influence must not assume that boldness, assurance, human wisdom, enthusiasm, and Weberian charisma embody power-giving. Neither must the laity or followership passively assign all responsibility to the leader: rather, each member must see themselves a part of a whole, creating a community with "a comprehensive range of gifts and resources, all lavished upon them as a corporeity or plurality to be used without picking and choosing the gifts."[7]

Rather than striving for another person's gift, each invests their own to the fullest extent, enabling others to do the same.

---

7. Thiselton, *First Epistle to the Corinthians*, 326.

Redeemed power goes against the rationality of social power theories; in fact, those power theories would become non-functional as viable theories if power were habitually exercised in a redeemed way. Redeemed power is (1) the capacity and ability to act (*dynamis*) made possible by Spirit baptism, physical strength, talents, and intellectual and material resources that have been developed through discipline and maturity; and (2) the freedom (*exousia*) made possible when the community recognizes the Spirit's gifts in individual members and creates space for them to develop their gifts and to function in service to others. Redeemed power is embodied in redeemed agents invested in a lifestyle of self-emptying for the sake of others.

The theology and practice of power in the inner life of believers will be revealed in public and social relationships. The sum of the individuals' spirituality creates the power-giving or power-keeping personality of the community of faith. When redeemed individuals, both leaders and followers, employ power in a redeemed way, the patterns of power, whether shaped in a more hierarchical or egalitarian way, will be centrifugal, focused on making space for all to serve as gifted members in the mission. Problems develop when there is no possibility in the DNA of a church to change the power relationships that have been entrenched in tradition. A dynamic, power-giving social organization will allow the church to be liquid, to mold into new forms as it crosses cultural and generational borders, faces the challenge of new tasks, and welcomes maturing, Spirit-gifted members into its decision-making circles.

Power-Giving Leadership Effects Liquid Restructuring

Unlike Church B, Church C has navigated the cultural change from hierarchical authoritarian to a more egalitarian, shared leadership structure without exchanging the pastoral leadership roles for democratic consensus. Several factors enabled them to accomplish this task.

First, Church C has had a long season of power-giving leadership under Pastor C. In the beginning of his ministry, he too adopted an authoritarian role, making structural changes that insured that the pastor was the "leader" (in contrast to many churches of that time where an elder was considered the head of the church). However, analysis today reveals that the majority of the members describe him as a consensus style leader with a passion for unity. It would be mistaken to see him as non-directive or non-persuasive, but he uses his position to make room for others to minister and flourish. A former elder noted to me that in Pastor C placed significant emphasis on unity and consensus. That is, it was not nor ever was democratic. He would work until unity and a sense of being one in the spirit. This particular pastor had the gift of convincing. He was able to create consensus though different opinions did exist. Sometimes, Pastor C would lay aside a topic for weeks, or even months for prayer and further consideration if necessary.

Second, Pastor C has consistently expanded the number of leadership roles, released members to envision and be in charge of ministry, and created fluid organizational structures (patterns of power) as the size and mission of the church grew. He invited members to participate in these structural transformations. Recently, pastors and members dedicated twelve hours to the examination of Scriptures to discover roles and spiritual characteristics of elders and deacons, examine varieties of structures portrayed in the New Testament, and discuss the leadership needs in their context.

Third, members have grasped that the church exists because of their mission to their city. Members are embedded in community relationships, understand the cultural changes taking place, and embrace their city as an arena for the Spirit's action. As a result, 85 percent of the many ministries into the community are driven by vision that was initiated from the laity in response to the local context of their lives. A community gospel choir, a youth center, a mother-child center for Muslim families, discussion groups for unemployed, and a choir to sing at grave-side funerals represent part of the many activities birthed in the heart of lay people of this congregation.

A complex scheme of roles and responsibilities divided among many people establishes a hierarchy; nonetheless, the main pastor, and therefore all the church's leadership, understands that they serve to empower others. The church avoids a power-keeping and power-striving posture in favor of an "empowered-together" stance, which creates an environment of communion rather than contesting. Laity and pastors alike understand the church to be a shared community, where leadership is well defined, but focused on recognizing vision and gifts in members and creating space for them to serve. In turn, members, perceiving that their voices and visions for mission are integral to the whole, love, respect, and support the leadership in the task God has given them for the sake of the community. Often members express the fact that although they do not agree with all decisions, they must "work together" to accomplish the mission.

Finally, the power relationships within the community speak prophetically to the cultural context. Pastor C has built trust in leadership in a culture that legitimizes egalitarianism and independence. Un-insulated, low Power Distance relationships characterize the church leadership and the structure patterns of power morph with the changing demographics of their city. Trust is palpable in the community, so that their life together critiques the independent, individualistic culture, even as it offers the hope of healthy relationships that are so desired, but feared in society. The Church functions as a community of "resident aliens" in a culture groaning for transformation; the way the Church organizes itself in each particular culture and setting must be prophetic, bearing the Good News in her relational structures.

Conclusion: The Power to Navigate Molten Times

The Church exists in molten times: ethnicities, value systems, and ideologies rub shoulders and clash together in the church's backyard. Generations slip away and economies rise and fall; therefore, the leadership of the church must encourage members to become biblically literate and cultural exegetes, in order to be transformed into a missional force in the next epoch of church history. As demonstrated by Church B and C, ecclesiological structure is not shaped purely by theological consideration; on the contrary, life together in a community of faith is born out of dynamic tension between the actors, the culture, and a biblical understanding of what it means to be church. Within leadership lies the responsibility to model, teach, and implant a DNA of redeemed power in such a way that the structures remain fluid, preventing a concretized form that may serve the present generation well, but will suffocate the next, inhibiting their capacity to face ever-developing challenges. A dynamic theology of power that anchors the community through changing times will quell the addiction of power-striving and foster an attitude of power-giving and self-sacrifice as the whole community is empowered to thrive in their context.

6

Generosity and Reciprocity in Thai Society

LARRY S. PERSONS

Patron-client patterns exert powerful influence in circles of leadership and followership in contemporary Thailand.

Leaders gain the cooperation of followers by mastering patterns of social exchange. These swirls of reciprocal obligations lend fertile insights into contests for power that occur daily between leaders as patrons and followers as clients. When we dig into those modes of reciprocity, we quickly encounter a Thai word of incredible significance and power: *bunkhun*.

Bunkhun is a deeply indigenous social phenomenon that continues to shape the fiber of most, if not all relationships in Thai society.

What is bunkhun a nutshell? Two abstract concepts form its meaning: "merit" and "virtue."

No single English word, however, does justice to the sublime layers of meaning enveloped by this social construct. It is relational reciprocity triggered by generosity. It emerges in a relationship when a person does something to benefit someone else and the grateful recipient feels a desire to reciprocate. This powerful construct therefore, falls solidly under the rubric of social exchange.

Thai social psychologist Dr. Suntaree Komin describes this as "a psychological bond between someone who, out of sheer kindness and sincerity, renders another person the needed helps and favors, and the latter's remembering of the goodness done and his ever-readiness to reciprocate the kindness."[1]

The Thai word for such gratitude is *katanyuu katawethi*, which one Thai scholar translates as "to remember and eventually reciprocate."

Yet, the English word "remember" does not fully capture the social richness of this term. "Loving indebtedness expressed through grateful behavior" is closer to the mark.

Bunkhun developed in the context of asymmetrical relationships nurtured by profound social disparity in ancient Thai society. Feudal patterns (*rabob jao khun moon naay*) dictated that those with economic power or authority to rule had very large entourages under their control and influence. When clients received protection and care, they found ways to reciprocate toward their benefactor (*phuu mee phrakhun*). These clients were at the service of the benefactor, and often their loyalty so consuming that they were willing to die for the patron. Such patterns were prominent in the patron-client systems of the early Bangkok period (1782–1873), when it held much the same meaning as it does today.

It is vital to acknowledge that this form of social exchange emanated from a context of reciprocity between persons of unequal power and status. Thai society is still based upon the feudal system where there are "big people" (*phuuyai*) and "little people" (*phuulek*). Though egalitarian forms of *bunkhun* appear in contemporary Thai society, most social exchange still reflects differences in hierarchy that have ancient roots. This indicates that *bunkhun* has everything to do with asymmetrical leadership processes that pervade modern Thailand on a daily basis.

Anyone who accepts an act of kindness in a time of need clearly relinquishes power to that patron. That person must "give face" to the benefactor on a regular basis. It is as though a person receives a loan and chooses to live in social indebtedness. Rarely is anything put into writing, so such relational calculus is often unclear if, when, or how the debt might be fully repaid. This explains the longevity that is characteristic of relational debt in Thai society. Sometimes that indebtedness feels light. Sometimes it feels heavy. Sometimes it can be repaid over time, and if so, the client can break free from the power of the patron. However, one of the most striking things about gratitude created by an act of *bunkhun* is how long it can endure in the heart of a client. What goes around truly does come around, and it continues to do so often for long periods.

1. Komin, *Psychology of the Thai People*, 1–2.

Persons—Generosity and Reciprocity in Thai Society

"Patron-based behavior is a matter of affection, relationship, and friendship," says a university professor in Bangkok. "But how do people live out its principles?"[2] That is a pivotal question. It acknowledges the reality that there are divergent social manifestations of *bunkhun* in Thai society. It is the start of a fruitful path of analysis that reveals two antipodal forms of the same dynamic.

Relational indebtedness, a congenital component of *bunkhun*, plays a powerful role in Thai leadership dynamics. An act of *bunkhun* always creates debt. The more Thais speak about reciprocity, the more it becomes clear that there exist two categorically different approaches to this system of social indebtedness. One patron doles out affection with little calculation and no intent to manipulate. The other gives with strings attached, making an investment from which he expects to reap a return. Both approaches begin with an act of generosity that puts *bunkhun* into motion. However, these forms of "kindness" are so expressly different that they generate two drastically different patterns of social exchange.

These feelings of indebtedness can vary significantly. "On the one hand, both parties are sincere in giving to each another," explains a university professor. "On the other hand, the patron wants to help but the client feels burdened. If he doesn't reciprocate, he will feel very uneasy. Both clients feel indebted to their patron, but they experience that indebtedness in very different ways."[3] The first feels affection and devotion. The second struggles with feelings of being manipulated.

What are the factors that determine such disparate feelings? How is it that *bunkhun* can be experienced so differently? In discussions regarding *bunkhun*, Thais refer to diluted or counterfeit forms. They use the phrase "false *bunkhun*" when a benefactor makes a move to his own advantage, hoping to gain something valuable in return for his generosity. This form of "*bunkhun*" represents instrumental social exchange—a contest of power between exchange partners—and nothing more.

In contrast, many speak of "*genuine bunkhun*" or "*righteous bunkhun*," a relationship that stirs good faith and true sincerity between exchange partners. The patron in this "morally pure" form of generosity gives something valuable to a client in a time of true need. This is done willingly, not out of compulsion, and because the patron truly likes and desires to help the recipient. Such becomes a gift of affection without conscious consideration

---

2. Unpublished interview with the author, October 25, 2005.
3. Unpublished interview with the author, October 25, 2005.

of what the patron might receive in return. There is no contractual agreement demanding reciprocity. This free act of kindness generates a feeling of loving indebtedness in the recipient.

What is clear is that despite the competitive, cutthroat leadership arenas of contemporary Thailand, altruism is alive and well. However, it is important to not become overly naïve. Calculated acts of social exchange are likely far more common in human relationships than forms of benevolent altruism. No social actor is likely free of all extrinsic social exchange forces. Especially in highly collectivist Thai society, social sanctions wield heavy influence on face behaviors, and such "face concerns" often significantly determine acts of kindness. It is critical to realize that *bunkhun* is rarely simply a private transaction between two people. Frequently there are others aware of the social transaction, and these become part of the equation as well. Sometimes a patron does not feel like assisting a potential client but must do so in order to maintain the face of the patron. If the patron does nothing for the subordinate, others might whisper to each other, gossiping about why the patron will not help others. Leaders who practice affectionate *bunkhun* are not immune to this social pressure to be generous. Even when patrons feel entirely altruistic in expressing a certain kindness, they may be unaware of the full scope and complexities of personal motives.

These Thai voices are significant enough to bid us to shed our cynicism regarding the possibility of altruism long enough to believe in a notion called "real *bunkhun*." When Thais speak of "real" *bunkhun* or "morally right/righteous" *bunkhun*, they claim that *bunkhun* must be kept from contamination or it can become a different thing altogether. That is, certain patterns of exchange in Thai society today are so far from the original essence of *bunkhun* they do not deserve the label.

It becomes polemical and counterproductive to insist on an idyllic, pure form of *bunkhun* that disqualifies contaminated expressions of this relational pattern. Since Thais use the word to describe both patterns of generosity and indebtedness, it seems better to think of *bunkhun* as a continuum of relational behaviors of similar ilk but with differing dynamics at each point along the way. This continuum would place affectionate bunkhun on one end with instrumental bunkhun on the other. Indeed, it is often difficult to judge the quality of a given display of *bunkhun*. Since some exchanges seem to be a blend of the two polar approaches to interaction, it is more helpful to identify two kinds of generosity with differing approaches to patron-client exchange. Here I draw a clear distinction between an

Persons—Generosity and Reciprocity in Thai Society

uncalculated act of kindness and an act that expects a client to reciprocate in a manner that is profitable for the patron.

At the far ends of the continuum are two divergent types of social exchange that look deceptively similar. On the one end, there is pristine affectionate *bunkhun*. On the other end is instrumental *bunkhun*, typified by *rabob upatham*, an ancient patron-client archetype with mercenary qualities that retains poignant influence over asymmetrical matchups in contemporary Thai society. Each approach to social exchange is a fully indigenous form of patron-client behavior.

If an act of uncalculated kindness is magnificent and substantial, most Thai clients sense a moral obligation to offer their patron reverence, obedience, and loyalty. If a client is a "good person," she will often embrace a debt that can never be repaid. She will be ready to do anything for the patron for the rest of his life.

Ideally speaking, the characteristics of affectionate *bunkhun* are as follows:

- The patron performs an act of kindness by doing something significant for a client that the client, in a time of need, cannot do alone.

- The act of the patron is willful and spontaneous. The giving is free from the coercion of others.

- The act of the patron is sincere. The motive in assisting is other-centered, intends to show kindness, or moral goodness, not to reap some benefit in return.

- These clients feel indebted. There is an awareness that the client likely cannot reciprocate toward the patron in like kind, and may never be able to pay the patron back in full.

- These feelings of client indebtedness are a warm thing. Because the client experiences genuine kindness as the object of patron generosity, a deep affection toward the patron is generated. This affection is enduring.

- The client responds with a lifelong pattern of spontaneous and sincere acts of kindness, both tangible (small gifts, favors) and intangible (obedience, loyalty, respect, love, praise and gratitude). This motivation for such behavior is *intrinsic*, not extrinsic. That is, these things are done not because clients must do them, but because clients *want* to do them. Clients feel genuine affection and deference toward the patron. This intrinsic, inside-out dynamic is a critical feature of this approach to social exchange.

Curiously, some kinds of indebtedness actually catalyze a cycle of relational warmth that many Thais crave. "True" *bunkhun* can influence behavior as long as both parties remain alive, and sometimes even longer. "We must engrave this in our hearts for our lifetime, and we must tell it to our children and grandchildren," explains one religious leader.[4] The Thai have a saying that nails this point: "Indebtedness to *bunkhun* can never be eaten away."

There exist many streams of social dynamics at work in Thai social exchange, however. One clear option is for a leader to learn the various cycles of reciprocity well and calculatedly play them to personal advantage. This approach represents a very different strain of generosity, viz., instrumental *bunkhun*.

A Thai judge vividly portrays this contrasting approach:

> Someone with 'prestige' and 'public acclaim' will build influence over people for the sake of his own personal profit. We call it "building up your arms and legs" so that you can increase in power. He *must* build up his subordinates so they can benefit him in the future. If he doesn't, he's dead, he's finished. You don't become capable or prominent all by yourself. You must have close subordinates under your control.[5]

The characteristics of instrumental *bunkhun* stand in stark contrast to affectionate *bunkhun*. What are the contours of this pattern of exchange?

- The patron performs an act of assistance by doing something significant for a client that the client, in a time of need, cannot do alone.
- It is a premeditated act. The patron may or may not be coerced into giving assistance.
- It is a calculated act designed to create indebtedness in the client. The motive in assisting is self-centered, with a view to reaping some benefit in return. This social investment "purchases" the loyalty and assistance of the client. The patron expects to collect on that investment sometime in the future.

---

4. Unpublished interview with the author, October 20, 2005.
5. Unpublished interview with the author, October 23, 2005.

- The client feels indebted. There is awareness that it is unlikely that the client can pay the patron back in like kind, and wonders if fully repaying the patron will be possible.
- The feelings of indebtedness in the client create a burdensome heaviness. Because the generosity is rooted in calculation, the client may feel manipulated and a loss of freedom. If the client senses ulterior motives, there may occur a significant effort to repay the debt once and for all. The *bunkhun* then loses its effect. Often, however, the calculus of repayment is kept so vague that a client can never be sure of just how much is enough.
- The client responds, either sincerely or grudgingly, with required acts of assistance, both tangible (small gifts, favors) and intangible (obedience, loyalty, respect, love, praise and gratitude). The motivation for doing so is *extrinsic*, not intrinsic. The client does these things because out of social compulsion, not out of genuine freedom. The client may reciprocate out of fear of the consequences of failing to respond properly. This outside-in pressure on the client is a quintessential characteristic of instrumental *bunkhun*.

An awkward sense of indebtedness settles upon victims of calculated kindness. "If a Thai patron performs *bunkhun* just once on behalf of a client, he fears that the patron is going to ask for reciprocation many, many times," says an office worker. "The client feels like he is perpetually indebted, yet he feels ungrateful if he does not reciprocate."[6]

Few Thais like this feeling of obligation. A religious teacher explains a common reluctance to accept favors: "It is like a circuit. Someone does something nice for you, but then one day you're going to have to pay him back. That's why I have some friends who don't want to accept big favors, because they're afraid of the payback."[7]

A retired government employee describes the uneasiness clients sometimes feel when they suspect that their patrons practice instrumental *bunkhun*:

> When I was a government worker, each year we would be promoted one level and granted a raise. The boss had authority to promote a limited quota of workers two levels at once, and he would usually grant this to whomever he thought had a heavy work load

---

6. Unpublished interview with the author, September 27, 2005.
7. Unpublished interview with the author, October 5, 2005.

or assisted him the most. One year I received it and I knew that I had to go thank my boss, but I was in conflict because I thought, "Hey, is this because of the boss's goodness, or is it something I deserve? Is this promotion a matter of *bunkhun*?" I didn't want to grovel in thankfulness for fear that he would think that he now had a special right to claim something from me. But I didn't want to be viewed as a subordinate who was hard-hearted and didn't know *bunkhun* either. So I just went and politely said thank you. But I was so afraid he would view it as *bunkhun* and I would lose freedom.[8]

Leadership and Bunkhun

Leaders create frames of influence by using the principles of instrumental *bunkhun*. They have power to draw people into their web by extending help to them. But once the kindness of a leader creates indebtedness in a relationship with a client, that leader gains significant control of the client. If there are only a few people in a local area who are not within his frame, the leader may pressure them. On the other hand, if more and more people begin to slip outside of this frame of influence, others may cease to comply with leader wishes resulting in the leader eventually losing social power.

Consider a community agricultural cooperative founded by a group of villagers in a rural district of Chiangmai province. They have pulled away from the influence of certain leaders in the community—not to set themselves up as enemies, but to bring greater justice to the average person. Their efforts are succeeding; so many villagers are exiting the frames of influence of certain leaders and coming over to their cooperative. The secret, we are told, is to establish independent organizations that do not hope for selfish profit, and then to think of ways to pass profits on to the collective. "It was very difficult at first because we had to prove that our intentions were noble," says a member of the coop committee. "But after a while when our alternative began to shine, people exited the old frames and entered the cooperative. The influence of former leaders disappeared. This is what a good society is like."[9]

When a client senses that his patron is taking advantage of him, he may attempt to find and secure another patron who is good-hearted, someone who may still gain advantage over others, but in a restrained way. Yet,

8. Unpublished interview with the author, October 21, 2005.
9. Unpublished interview with the author, October 16, 2005.

Persons—Generosity and Reciprocity in Thai Society

as one villager laments, "Sometimes you can't get away. It is like fleeing a tiger to meet up with a crocodile."[10]

In cities across the country, powerful patrons offer "security" to local people. Even honest shopkeepers must comply because they need security. They will reciprocate with payments of money or other economic opportunities that are potentially beneficial to the patron, such as granting partial ownership in their business or company.

Leaders make use of instrumental *bunkhun* to climb the hierarchical structures within Thai society. A former government worker explains:

> The patron-based system is about profiting in some way—both parties profit or benefit. The superior gains certain benefits from below that will continue to push him upward. His acts of generosity give him stability so that he can do many, many things. He must share profits with those below him, of course, so that they will maintain the things he desires from them. But it's a sure thing that he doesn't want to stay just where he is in the hierarchy. He wants to climb. Even if he has reached the top position of leadership, he still wants those below him to "give him a sense of place," you see, to continue to affirm where he stands and how he performs in his work. He must nurture a certain group of people to support his own stability. And those willing to receive the care of a patron are always hoping to receive benefits from their superior, right? It's like that, and it involves more than just one or two levels of leadership. It's this way through long strings of patron-client relationships in the hierarchy.[11]

To gain employment often takes the help of a person with influence. "All it takes is a call from him to the right people, and we have the job. But then we owe him," says a professor at Khonkaen University.[12] Consider a young man who must take the government exam to get a job at the Customs Department. Only one out of every 10,000 who take the exam will qualify. He takes the exam, and he's one of a group of ten people selected for a job interview. When he notices that others are being called for interviews before him, he talks with his father, a government worker who knows a certain cabinet minister.

---

10. Unpublished interview with the author, October 16, 2005.
11. Unpublished interview with the author, October 23, 2005.
12. Unpublished interview with the author, October 30, 2005.

> His father says, "There is actually more than one job open, but the better jobs are going first. See, to get this kind of a job you need to know someone. If you want me to, I'll talk to my friend, and you'll have the job, no question. But you understand, don't you, son, that from now on you will be indebted to this man's *bunkhun*. And once you get the job, if he sends someone to ask if you can 'help' him, you will have no choice but to help. I'd like you to be free of that reciprocal circuit. So you can either take the short-cut, or you can wait out your chances." The young man decides to wait it out instead, and he lands a good job anyway.[13]

Patrons often promote members of their own entourage to titled positions. Once attaining positions through the help of a patron, these clients must reciprocate for the *bunkhun* that has been shown to them. This cronyism is typical of instrumental *bunkhun*, and there is a growing feeling among educated Thais that this has caused Thailand to develop slowly. In good management, the manager knows who shows true ability and who does not. There is a verification process for making promotions. "But in this system it's like, 'My people are good. All others are bad,'" says a retired member of the Royal Thai Air Force, mimicking a patron. "Gifted candidates who don't practice instrumental *bunkhun* will not rise to higher levels of leadership. Those who rise are those who reciprocate and do favors for others, yet often they are not as gifted. This is why the country develops slowly. For the most part, instrumental *bunkhun* dictates the outcome of promotions in leadership."[14]

Typically, a patron has power of money, understanding that to gain face and power the patron must secure a reputation of being generous. This creates the appearance of a large entourage of loyal followers. "When a politician functions this way, it is a matter of maintaining his votes for the next election," says a government employee.[15]

Clients, therefore, often comply for the sake of money and are not sincere about the relationship. A government employee explains:

> If you are very wealthy, and you give me a large sum of money, and I turn around and give it to my entourage of sixteen people, 10,000 baht each per month, whenever I return to see you, these sixteen have to come along as well, you see? If just twelve come, you'll ask, "Who are the other four?" And next time those four get nothing.

13. Unpublished interview with the author, October 5, 2005.
14. Unpublished interview with the author, October 8, 2005.
15. Unpublished interview with the author, October 9, 2005.

> They are excommunicated. They lose their opportunity. And the remaining members say, "Hey, if we don't look after our grand patron, he'll cut the flow of money. No way I'm doing that!"[16]

Patrons must continue providing advantages and benefits to their entourages or they risks losing clients to other patrons. If they don't take care of their own, others may judge them as being "narrow-hearted" and stingy. The next time there is an election or a power struggle, they lose.

The way for a leader to negotiate his ascension in a hierarchy is to make use of principles of indebtedness. If a leader practices a lifestyle of being good to those less advantaged—consistently living the principles of affectionate *bunkhun* over a period of many years—subordinates may begin to say that the leader has "accumulated goodness" (*baramee*). If subordinates feel that assistance is given with ulterior motives, they will acknowledge the kindness of the superior only so long as they remain under his authority or his command. A policeman shares this anecdote:

> At one time, a very high-ranking officer in the air force used his power excessively. He did not show grace—we Thai use the word *khun*. All he used was power (*pradech*). He didn't show kindness (*prakhun*). He didn't help anyone at all. The smallest infraction, he would make a big deal of it. He punished his subordinates harshly. Even cases that should have been treated lightly, he heaped on the heaviness. One day he retired and went to play golf at the Air Force links. He ran into his old subordinates, and they acted like they couldn't care less. They spit in his direction and spewed sarcastic words. That man had no more meaning because he was retired. No one was interested in playing golf with him. He was nobody—just an old man. He had no 'accumulated goodness,' none at all.[17]

A negative aspect of instrumental *bunkhun* is the tunnel vision that clients often adopt in indiscriminately reciprocating for the good that a patron has done for them. Consider the case of a long-time congressman who decides to have his son run for congress. Many who have granted patron-like status to the congressman feel obligated to support his son, regardless of his true qualifications. "They'll get him elected, give him their acceptance, give him 'prestige,'" says a judge. "But they don't love the son. It's the father they love, respect and fear. They must support him."[18]

16. Unpublished interview with the author, October 8, 2005.
17. Unpublished interview with the author, October 25, 2005.
18. Unpublished interview with the author, October 23, 2005.

Citizens often vote for the candidate to whom they feel the most indebted, not for the most capable or virtuous candidate. This creates a large opening for patrons who wish to subvert the honor system. If they can create indebtedness in others, their clients feel strong social sanction to comply with their wishes. Leaders can buy "prestige."

When certain powerful patrons express their wishes, clients feel forced to offer implicit obedience and unbridled cooperation. Patrons may ask them to break the law, knowing that their indebted clients must comply. A banker explains:

> A lot of times personal obligations supersede what is lawful. Suppose you hit a pedestrian with your car and kill him. If you know someone, when the police report comes out, it's distorted in your favor.[19]

This focus on the vested interests of patrons and clients is native to instrumental *bunkhun*. It is a power struggle. Patrons use clients to protect assets and expand power. Clients are pressured to look after their patron's interests, but at the same time, they steadfastly pursue their own interests. If a client steps out of line or damages a patron's vested interests, the patron will often exact revenge.

So there are two distinct yet confluent social practices of *bunkhun* that have much in common. The patron does something for the client that the client cannot do alone. This act of generosity gives the patron power over the client. The client feels a sense of indebtedness, and in most cases reciprocates in ways that are beneficial to the patron. Yet, the two approaches are profoundly distinct. The difference in these models of reciprocity originates in each patron's motives for assisting his client. One gives to gain personally from accumulated largesse. The other is generous out of genuine empathy, demonstrating a type of kindness with no strings attached. This critical variable is subtle, yet profoundly dictates the entire range of dynamics in each model.

The contrast between feelings of indebtedness in respective clients is also captivating. One response is reluctant and sometimes fearful. The other is loving and spontaneous. Both of these approaches to exchange can be productive, but the relationship established through affectionate *bunkhun* is more stable and enduring.

It is advisable to keep in mind, however, that these two approaches, extremes on the far ends of a continuum, are not mutually exclusive choices.

---

19. Unpublished interview with the author, October 24, 2005.

Persons—Generosity and Reciprocity in Thai Society

It is likely that most acts of *bunkhun* are a blend of the two. The millions of manifestations of *bunkhun* in Thai society fall at divergent points along that line. However, it is difficult, if not impossible, to "map" a given relationship along that continuum. In fact, a patron's motive for assisting is a vital variable. Attempting to judge the full and true motives of any person, however, is an exceedingly tenuous exercise that can be prone to much error.

Still, we can be certain of one thing: *bunkhun* commands a powerful influence upon relationships in contemporary Thai society. "You have a giver and a receiver," says a retired banker. "The one who gives more is the leader. The one who must depend upon the other is the follower."[20] There is no doubt that an act of *bunkhun* can award significant power to the giver. It can create a sense of dependency that sustains power for long periods.

This pattern of generosity and reciprocity has profound implications for how leaders gain face and use power. Because patron-client models still prevail in most displays of Thai leadership and followership, we would all do well to exercise judgment in recognizing each leadership process for what it really is. "A leader is like a large *poh* tree that gives shade," explains a university professor. "Followers are like birds who perch on branches of the tree."[21] But a leader can choose between two very different approaches to extending the shade of his provision. Facework between a leader and his followers is likely to differ significantly depending upon the leader's deepest motives for broadening power and influence over others. For followers, the perch on one tree can feel quite different from the perch on another. One feels tenuous and somewhat dangerous. The other feels warm and secure.

---

20. Unpublished interview with the author, October 24, 2005.
21. Unpublished interview with the author, October 30, 2005.

7

Activating Kingdom Agents
Toward a Model of Awakening and Releasing God's People For Ministry and Leadership

ALAN WEAVER

Pastor Lajos has seven youth groups, and 12 youth leaders. I was impressed. Each year he taught the confirmation class of 13 year-olds. At the end of the year, he turned over the class to a nervous young couple who would then stick with this group of young people for the next several years as their youth leaders. Year after year the process would be repeated till now there were seven youth groups. What intrigued me was not the number of groups, but the number of young leaders whom he had pulled into ministry.

But this was not the exciting part of the church. The congregation buzzed about the upcoming "all-ages" camp that the church puts on every summer. In this camp, they said that more growth took place in one week than took place in half a year. Professionals or paid staff did not run the camp, but church members planned and ran the whole week. Twenty-five small groups required many new leaders to try their hand at ministry, often for the first time. Music leaders tried out new music on an appreciative audience, while each night a different group would be responsible for the worship service and message for the evening meeting. The older folks were amazed at the depth of spirituality expressed by the younger generations, while the young people came to appreciate the years of wisdom and breadth that came with older years. All came to appreciate one another.

When all was done, the leaders of the camp, now participating in various leadership roles and ministries in the church, met once a quarter to discuss the church's ministry and learn from debriefing one another. Through this program and others like it, a new spirit has entered the church as laity embraced their own call to service. Several new and creative ministries have emerged as laity discover new ways to reach their community and serve one another.

Pastor Lajos is a pastor who seems to have attained the ideal to which many pastors only aspire, the ideal which Ephesians 4:11–12 calls leaders to do, "to equip saints for the work of ministry." But he is not alone. In Hungary, I studied several growing churches from different Christian traditions (Reformed, Baptist, and Charismatic) which were all experiencing a rapid rise in the number of laity who were not only becoming active in ministry but also emerging as leaders. Church members felt excited and empowered; they knew that what was happening in their churches was unusual.

These churches were all the more remarkable in Hungary, which had only a decade earlier thrown off the old communist regime that sought to downsize the church and to limit the church to the four walls of the building and to the work of one person. Pastor after pastor explained that communist overseers only allowed licensed clergy to do any ministry in the church, and even then, activities were limited. Over the decades, this oppression sowed seeds of passivity and helplessness, especially among the members of the congregation that many pastors found difficult to overcome. The church was quietly being suffocated, and this trend was continuing despite the fact that the oppressors had long gone.

The challenge that the church faced is similar to what pastors all over the world face: how do you move the people of God from being fans in the stands to players on the field? How do you unlock their God-given gifts and potential to become agents of the Kingdom of God?

A Question of Agency

The term "leadership emergence" succinctly expresses the popular desire for new leaders to be raised up visibly and prominently in churches. However, such an understanding may cause some to focus on certain aspects of leadership more closely associated with charismatic leaders rather than on those people who are quietly, but consistently, making a difference in their group. Such also does not fully recognize the fluidity of leadership roles; that is, people act as leaders at some points and as followers at other points, even within the same group. Indeed, some of the most desired traits in followers are also traits recognized as important to leadership.

In short, it is difficult to recognize who is an emerging leader, especially while they are in the process of emerging.

It is at this point that the term "agency" becomes useful. It raises the issue of how people begin to distinguish themselves from their surrounding culture, not simply be participants in that culture but become shapers of it. In the early phases of leadership emergence, people often are not recognized either by themselves or by others as leaders, but they are learning to be agents in their environment. The more effective they are as agents, the more likely they will be recognized, in fact, as leaders. Though I am clearly interested in leadership emergence, I find that the word agency is often more useful and I use it conspicuously in this article.

Sociologists Anthony Giddens and Margaret Archer discuss the concept of agency through the lens of individual autonomy and action.[1] Both defend the idea that human beings are not programmed by their environment and culture, but are complex creatures, which are able to make decisions and act independently. At the same time, they recognize that society and the environment must be taken into account. As an advocate of "social realism" Archer affirms the environment's contribution (both society's and the natural world's) to provide the context and conditioning of a decision, though not determining it, retaining full human autonomy.

What are the environmental factors that contribute to the emergence of God's people into ministry and leadership? For the last several centuries, the Western church has focused largely on education as the primary way to develop competent workers and leaders to minister in the church. Yet, most of us would recognize that not all those who are educated become active in ministry, while others become strong Christian leaders without much training at all. Realizing that more was involved in how people emerged as agents and leaders, I began to ask the question, "What are the environmental factors that stimulate agency and allow people to actually begin to contribute to the work and leadership of the church?"

To answer this question, I studied six churches that had reputations for having a large percentage of lay leaders for churches their size. Churches

1. Archer, *Being Human*, 7–12.

were chosen from three Protestant traditions: two Hungarian Reformed, two Hungarian Baptist, and two independent charismatic. My case studies included observations of church life, interviews with the pastor, and a congregational survey. But the critical part of the study revolved around the active interviews with 6–10 lay leaders from each church, a total of 44 informants. I usually met with each person twice and explored his or her leadership development history and the factors that contributed to their emergence as leaders.

As a check on my results, I interviewed ten pastors of more average churches, where leaders were not notably emerging. These were my control churches. In addition, one of the six "model" churches I studied turned out to be more a model of church growth than leadership growth: a situation in which a nearly dead church had been resurrected to life through the efforts of a strong pastor but was not yet producing lay leaders. Indeed, the authoritarian style of the pastor created problems for the leaders that did exist. This case study, along with the ten control churches, stood in contrast to the other five churches.

Despite the great difference in style, polity, doctrine and practice amongst the churches I studied, the critical factors in leadership emergence were remarkably similar. Their struggle to cast off the old enforced somnolence of the laity to morph into churches where members were creatively and powerfully using their gifts for ministry provides a unique opportunity to learn from their experiences.

Ministry Experience

It has become a truism that nothing teaches like experience. By far, people indicated that experience contributed the most to their emergence as leaders. They would often say that they learned to do their ministry in "deep waters"—thrown in without preparation or before they felt competent. Essential skills developed through the processes of trial and error, through trying to communicate, make decisions, and study the Bible, lead groups and through various ministry activities. People learned because they had to.

Besides skill development, experience was instrumental in the development of other agential characteristics such as those we now recognize as part of emotional intelligence.

Devoted to Christ

I was curious where people developed the passion and commitment to become involved in ministry. When asked this question, many again would point to experience, talking about a ministry experience they had which opened their eyes to the need of those they ministered to. Several women responded to the joy and excitement of the children with whom they worked and the gratitude that was expressed to them by the parents. Another man's heart for ministry began as a young man when he was taken along to help distribute food and clothes to the poor in neighboring Romania. Experience in ministry made people feel valuable, a part of something important, and helped them realize that they too could serve God.

Besides passion and commitment, a greater sense of responsibility also grew out of ministry experience. When a person was given responsibility for the care or leading of others, he or she took this seriously, worked harder and became more sensitive to the needs of others. A paradigm shift took place in which a person moved from passive receiver to caregiver. One person described the shift in thinking as similar to becoming a parent; one suddenly becomes absorbed in meeting the needs of others.

Through experience people became surer of their abilities and discovered things about themselves that changed their self-image. They discovered what they could, and sometimes, what they could not do. All of this gave them a new vision for their capabilities, gifts, and role in the Kingdom of God.

I watched this process take place in front of my eyes when I attended the summer camp in Lajos's church. At the camp, lay leaders pair up and lead small, age-based groups for the week. A young seminarian had joined the church and was given charge of a brand new youth group of recently confirmed 13 year-olds. At the beginning of the week he appeared nervous and uncertain, but later he showed excitement and animation about his experience. He shared with the co-workers fellowship at the camp debrief that he had been nervous because he had never seen a church camp before, never seen a church where laity did ministry, had never led a youth group before, did not know what to expect, and did not know if he could even relate to the kids. The week of intense ministry in which he could see the changes in the young people over the course of the week and see them respond to him personally opened his eyes to new possibilities. This experience not only gave him a better idea of what relational ministry was, but also helped him gain greater confidence in his ability to do ministry. It was easy to see why this camp was the high point in the development of group leaders in the life of the church.

Finally, experience had an important social component in the development of leaders. Almost all leaders had started in small ministries and worked up to larger ones. Many quoted 1 Timothy 5:22, in which Paul exhorts Timothy not to lay hands on a person quickly. Others quoted Luke 16:10, that "whoever can be trusted with very little can be trusted with much."

When I asked pastors and emerging leaders about how people became leaders in the church, they almost always mentioned the importance of having a ministry in which the congregation could see that a person was committed to the church and faithful in the carrying out of responsibilities. Activity demonstrated important character qualities such as commitment, faithfulness, responsibility, loyalty, and energy. Active people received greater opportunities to take on more significant responsibilities. So experience in ministry increased social credibility and trust that made ministry and leadership possible.

Sometimes the ministry role itself changed people's behavior to match the expectations of their new role. Role expectations caused emerging leaders to modify their behaviors to meet the role requirements. One melancholic youth leader learned that when he was in front of the young people he had to act more upbeat. Religious education teachers found that people came to them for advice about their children and so they had to learn to counsel them. Social role expectations are a part of the formation of many emerging agents and leaders.

Experience was so important to the pastors of these five churches that they intentionally sought to involve young Christians in ministry from their earliest moments as believers, whether in sharing their testimony or helping teach a Sunday School class. Teaching and training was important, but they felt that people grew more in the fires of experience than they did passively absorbing content. To their own amazement, their young leaders felt the same.

Structures of Opportunity

Related to experience, opportunity also played a key role in leadership emergence. James MacGregor Burns writes about "structures of opportunity" which refers to the organizational characteristics that make opportunity possible.[2]

Open structures offer many places for people to connect to ministry, while closed structures make ministry hard to find. Four of the five strong leadership emergence cultures had open structures of opportunity.

Open structures manifested themselves in two ways. First, a strong missional focus provoked a congregation to continually open new and creative ministries that required more human resources and new leadership. In two of the churches, a growing network of small groups gave opportunity for many to step into leadership. Most of the leaders I spoke to had opportunity to lead a small group of some kind. For three of the churches, opportunity for ministry and leadership opened through a continuous parade of creative evangelistic outreaches—a Christmas package program that had to be coordinated or an evangelistic drama held in a local theater, which involved most of the congregation. Mission both required and drove the development of agents.

New opportunities for ministry also opened up as part of the reorganization of church structures. I had the good fortune of arriving just in time to see a successful individualist style church make the transition into a hierarchical form of government. They had grown in number to the point where they needed more structure because their old ad hoc system of doing things allowed too many things and people to fall through the cracks. They created a new system of elders and deacons, which gave elders oversight of shepherding and major divisions of the church while creating a number of new positions for deacons to have oversight of smaller ministry areas. The reorganization of the leadership structure opened up new spaces for people to lead and doubled the number of leaders in a very short time.

In most cases qualified people already existed who were willing and available but who had not been leading merely because of a lack of opportunity. In many cultural contexts, it is not appropriate for people to create their own opportunities or to volunteer for ministry. Several leaders indicated that the pastor had to be the one to ask them to do something because to do otherwise would be considered presumptuous. In each case I studied, it was the pastor who had to take the initiative to open up space for his people because he was the one who had both the authority and the resources to create a new ministry opportunity.

---

2. Burns, *Leadership*, 427.

Interestingly, one church that had been rapidly growing was disconcerted that they were beginning to experience stagnation in their progress. When I examined their current structures of opportunity, I could see that the church had few new places where people could serve or lead. They had filled up the ministry positions and new ones were not being created. Leaders placed in positions earlier were beginning to get tired and lose steam while other potential leaders were not being tapped.

It is easy for a church or mission that has seen great success and growth to become blinded to the fact that their structures of opportunity are slowly reducing in number. Successful leaders who had earlier been given opportunity are not providing similar opportunities to others. If new leadership is to emerge and thrive, older structures often need to be opened up so that new growth can take place.

Pastoral Attitudes and Support

The role of the pastor in creating open structures of ministry opportunity and then supporting new leadership should not be underestimated. Significantly, all five of the pastors of the churches with leadership emergence cultures had a high view of laity and sought to involve them in the work of the Kingdom. One pastor saw his role as that of a tree trunk supporting the branches of a fruit tree. He emphasized that it is not the trunk that bears the fruit but the branches. The trunk provides support and a channel for nourishment.

Most of the informants recognized the pastor's role in involving them in service. Nearly all of them had been recruited by the pastor for a ministry at some point. Several specifically mentioned the importance of the pastor in recognizing their ability and potential even when they could not see it themselves.

Pastors played a particularly key role in the support of entrepreneurs—those emerging leaders with initiative and creativity who tried new things. Young leaders with fresh ideas were particularly vulnerable to the criticisms of older and more powerful church elders and leaders. In the case studies, all the pastors were rated highly by their young leaders in the area of being supportive and open to new ideas. Over half of the young leaders expressed great appreciation for how their pastors publicly supported them and sometimes protected them from the challenges of older leaders.

This often took courage and political finesse on the part of leadership. One pastor who came to a church with a reputation for intransigent traditionalism, managed to start a contemporary music group in the church by going to the elderly members and conspiratorially asking them to pray for these young people who were daring to try something new and risky in order to reach out to the youth in the community. He turned potential adversaries into tolerant and sometimes even enthusiastic supporters.

The oldest pastor I interviewed had been introducing changes in his churches for nearly six decades. He had the reputation of successfully activating laity in ministry in every church he had pastored. At 78, when I asked him about his leadership in introducing contemporary music into his worship services he said, "I always take the side of life, because life eventually conquers death."

Informants mentioned several other ways that their pastor's support was critical. Most felt the strong encouragement of their pastor at different times when their confidence faltered or when life conspired against them. For many leaders, the hours spent discussing their ministry with the pastor was key; for others leaders, the materials and the organizational structures the pastor provided were essential to their emergence as leaders. As an example, the pastor empowered one young mother by helping her find babysitters and people to help at home so that she could lead a youth group and also work with other young mothers in the community.

Pastor Lajos had a unique way of giving added authority and credibility to his young leaders before other members of the congregation. He would address these leaders with the informal title of respect, *bachi* (uncle) or *neni* (aunt). This resulted in some good-natured kidding when the new leader was maybe only 20 or 25 years old, but it did demonstrate that the pastor respected his or her work and considered them leaders.

In contrast, the pastors of more traditional churches that were not involving laity had decidedly clerical views of the role of pastor and congregants. Several that I talked to expressed the view that they themselves were the ones who were trained for ministry and had the necessary expertise, not the laity. As one put it, "I would let a construction engineer preach in my pulpit if he would then allow me to build his house." When I asked others if they would support small groups led by church members, their response was to ask what the point of it would be. They simply saw no need. These pastors were keeping the doors of opportunity firmly shut.

Community Support and Atmosphere

I expected that a healthy fellowship was important to church growth and well being. But I was surprised and intrigued when people rated qualities like family atmosphere and love and acceptance not only as strengths of the church, but also as important to leadership development and emergence.

Genuine love and acceptance allowed people to feel at home and secure. In one case, I found the group of emerging leaders that I interviewed to be very dissatisfied with various aspects of church life—yet they unanimously agreed that their church embraced people with strong levels of warmth and acceptance. Love covered a multitude of sins and made them want to stay, to continue to serve, and to lead. To paraphrase one young Hungarian pastor, service came naturally out of fellowship.

For many of the emerging leaders, the love and acceptance they found in the church and the encouragement and recognition they received there was a necessary support mechanism for their esteem needs—it generated hope for their future rather than melancholy or despair. It helped give them a new identity.

One man, aware of his worker class status in Hungarian society, said that he would never have been given a chance to grow and have a position of leadership without the accepting character of his church. He now manages a Christian bookstore. He went on to say that the family-like closeness was important in the church because personality forms in the context of one's family. Two young men mentioned that they had been shy and reclusive but that the love and acceptance they experienced in the church had turned their personalities upside down. To their surprise they now found themselves speaking to community leaders, initiating and putting together community outreaches and doing things they never would have dreamed of doing before.

In several churches, I noticed that leaders seemed to grow rapidly during periods in which they found strong camaraderie in either an informal group of like-minded committed believers or in a more formal group of likewise committed co-workers. In these groups the high level of commitment and morale seemed to sustain and feed the passion, excitement and commitment of all the members.

The members of Pastor Lajos's "co-worker's fellowship" coalesced as a working team during the church camp, but throughout the year they continued to meet with each other to discuss ideas about future ministry, share helpful books and tools they had come across, discuss current problems together, and offer counsel from their own experiences. Despite the technical expertise and competence that Pastor Lajos clearly had, these church leaders indicated that they actually learned more from one another than they did through their times with the pastor.

Though synergy and technical ministry support could be found in these working groups, it was the emotional support found there that seemed to mean the most to the emerging leaders. They enjoyed being together, working together, and the spiritual commitments they saw in others stimulated and challenged their own. The community itself became the mentor and source of inspiration to its members.

The importance of community may be one of the most overlooked aspects to development of agents for God's kingdom. One young man had lost a child and nearly washed out but for the support of his church. He likened his church to an aircraft carrier that he could return to for refueling and support during the battle. It is hard to imagine someone being effective in ministry, much less growing in leadership without having such a secure and nurturing base. But it is easy to take for granted until it is missing.

It is good to recognize again the role of pastoral leadership in the cultivation of this fellowship of co-workers. Pastor Lajos's leaders were quick to credit their pastor for assembling and empowering this fellowship. Sherwood Lingenfelter calls this "building a community of trust,"

which makes learning and accountability to one another possible. Pastor Lajos recognized that once the fellowship was established, his role had changed. He no longer had to be the one doing the ministry or even driving the people, rather his role was to provide vision, coordination, and support, "a different kind of work."

Spiritual Input

Spirituality is quite literally the heart and soul of the Christian leader. When I explored how people developed spiritually and how their commitment and relationship to God grew, many expressed it in terms of the grace of God at work in their heart to call them to a greater commitment and relationship with God. For some it came with signs of power, but even among the two charismatic churches informants felt that spiritual growth came primarily as a result of God's superintending work over a period of time. People expressed that spiritual growth came through the teaching of

God's Word, the spiritual modeling of his people, and various experiences in which God demonstrated his faithfulness to his children.

All of the pastors of my case studies had the ability to express spiritual truths in a relevant and clear manner. Though each had a distinct preaching style, all expressed a message with a strong spiritual ethos—people viewed their personal spirituality as genuine and inspiring and this gave weight to their teaching.

Christian models and mentors played a major role in the spiritual formation of most I interviewed. The pastor's own spiritual depth and passion spurred many people on to greater commitment. Besides the pastor, most people could point to several people in their lives that modeled Christian life and ministry for them. The exemplary lifestyle of these special men and women motivated the emerging agents to adopt their values and aspire to be like them.

Finally, faith grew as people had experiences both in their ministry and in their lives in which they could see that God was powerful and faithful. This increased their confidence and trust in Him. A few had experienced God walking with them through deep crises—for a couple of people this made them more sensitive to God and to other people, for a few others it made them re-examine their lives and their priorities.

Conclusion

The five factors I mentioned above (experience, opportunity, pastoral support, community support and spiritual inputs) all made both internal and external contributions to a person's agency. These played a significant role in a person's internal development, providing spiritual commitment and passion, a growing sense of responsibility, ministry and social skills, and confidence. At the same time, these factors were often important in providing an external environment that allowed and aided a person's effectiveness in making an impact on their environment, whether in providing opportunity and resources or social credibility and legitimacy. Certainly these case studies demonstrate the complexity of factors, which contribute to a person's agency and emergence as a leader.

I highlight two things that deserve special attention. First, much more was involved in emergence as agents and leaders than just academic training and input. This supports the contention of Edgar J. Elliston's that "training is important, but it is only one of many critical elements in facilitating the emergence of a leader."

The second observation is that agents come from a variety of backgrounds and are not predetermined by their social position. However, agents strongly benefit from a leader or community that is able to recognize and release their potential.

A model of agency requires several aspects working together to enervate the potentials of God's people. In this study, I have mentioned five factors that came to the forefront in the field research: ministry experience, structures of opportunity, pastoral attitudes and support, congregational attitudes and support, and spiritual inputs. Teaching and training also played a role, though never as a substitute for the transforming power of experience. Nevertheless, it and other components could be added to the model as other key influences contributing to agency. God operates through these and other factors in the distinctiveness of the individual to create and empower people who operate as unique agents of salt and light.

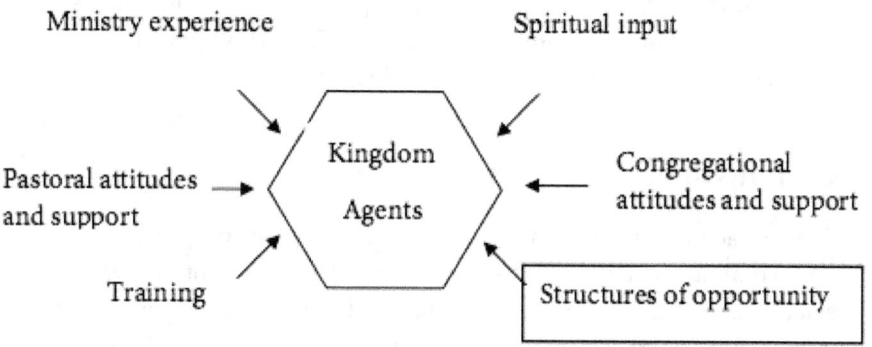

Figure 1. Toward a Model for Building Kingdom Agents

Those involved in helping churches and church leaders around the world equip people for ministry must not only take into account the training aspects of individual development, but also those aspects which cultivate a person's internal world of emotions, attitudes and commitments. Further, we need to be alert to those aspects of agency, which are dependent on the local church and leadership context. A more holistic model of agency may help us better cooperate with the work of God to develop the potential and release the power of his people as agents of his kingdom in the world.

Thanks to the following pastors and churches for their example and for giving me the opportunity to study their ministries: Lajos and Judit Püski of Nagyerdei Reformed Church, Géza Kovács of Kecskemét Baptist Church, Gyuri Kováts of Mahanaim Full Gospel Christian Fellowship, István Perjesi of the Agapé Fellowship, and Kálmán Mészáros of Székesfehérvár Baptist Church.

8

Leadership and Patron-Client Structures in Thailand

LORRAINE DIERCK

The complexity of cross-cultural communication continues to baffle and confuse people engaged in the task of frontier missions. A young missionary to Thailand said, "I came to Thailand with a big vision, and with a lot of skill and enthusiasm. I know I have a lot to contribute to this ministry. But the Thai leaders go ahead and do whatever they want without discussing anything with me. I feel totally useless. I'm planning to go back to England as soon as possible." For many expatriate mission partners, Thai leadership seems like a mysterious black box that is virtually impossible to decode. How does the Thai power structure work? How do Thai leaders make decisions? Who makes the decisions? What are the underlying values that influence Thai leaders? Who are the powerless? And the corollary to this—how do Thai mission partners view their expatriate partners, especially when those leaders seem to function like a mean, stingy boss with power but no compassion?

Mission partners often find that the cultural values underlying the patron-client environment powerfully influence social interactions between Thais and expatriate missionaries. To understand better how Thai leaders use power, some have applied the writings and theories of Dr. Sherwood Lingenfelter regarding the importance of cultural values and the difference between default cultural values and Biblical values. Cultural values reflect how groups of people perceive what is desirable, valuable and good within their culture. Missiologists define cultural values as any pattern or aspect of life that a given culture or subculture shares, and which therefore has worth, or value to them.

Cultural norms include all the values, expectations, and rules of a given social group, and they are automatic to people who share the same culture. The fact that outsiders have not found these responses automatic has contributed to the high level of stress that expatriate mission partners have often experienced.

Grid-group measurement is a cultural diagnostic tool that has shed light on the conventions governing the Thai social environment. Mary Douglas identified "grid" and "group" as being two social factors that identify the dimensions of the social life of any group of people that have ordered relationships.

Grid describes the structured place and role of individuals within a social activity, and the degree to which individuals are constrained by social rules. The concept of group indicates the degree to which individuals are embedded within social groups, particularly bounded social groups. According to Douglas, the combination of high and low values for the dimensions of grid and group produces a four-fold typology that describes the major forms of social organization. Thompson, Ellis, and Wildavsky further adapted the grid-group model to provide a typology for five possible ways of life: the fatalist, the hierarchist, the individualist, the egalitarian, and the hermit. Using these concepts, Lingenfelter proposes that grid and group give rise to five "prototype social games" that can also be used to describe a mission environment.

Therefore, while Lingenfelter did not originate the grid-group paradigm, he applies the concept in an original and accessible way for mission partners.

The Patron-Client System in Thailand

Thailand is one of the oldest, but most resistant, Protestant mission fields in Asia. The country was known as Siam until June 24, 1939, when it took the name Thailand, meaning "Land of the Free." Buddhism is the state religion, and archeological evidence shows that the Thai people have been Buddhist since at least the eleventh century.

Devoted to Christ

The growth of the church among the Thai people has remained slow right up to the present. One important factor that has contributed to the small number of converts is the strong link between royal power and religion. The Thai people demonstrate strong allegiance to their nation, Buddhism, and the monarchy, with the elements inextricably bound together so that devotion to any one of the three is equated with loyalty to all.

The Thai social system is arranged in a hierarchy of mutually beneficial relationships, leading to two categories of people: superior and inferior.

Norman Jacobs bluntly states that, "The patrimonial hierarchy of clients and patrons are the touchstone of Thai social relationships."

The relationship between superior and subordinate is predictable—the superior has benevolent, calmly self-assured and authoritative characteristics while the subordinate should be respectful, attentive, and helpful. Power accrues to those at the top of the chain, and those with less status expect their patron will exercise power to benefit both patron and client. The result of this system is inequality and power distance, "the extent to which the less powerful members of organizations and institutions accept and expect that power is distributed unequally."

Mission partners from lower grid cultures are perplexed when Thais expect, and even seem to prefer, hierarchical gaps between people in society.

The patron-client system in Thailand has its roots at least as far back as the eleventh century, when a system known as *sakdina* constituted an efficient chain of command that helped ethnic Thais register the population. At that time, constant warfare meant that the success of the state was dependent on mobilizing adequate labor resources to till the fields and enlist in the military during times of battle. The Thai response was to require every *phrai* (commoner) to register under a *nai* (master) who was responsible to lead those registered under him into battle at the command of the king. The *nai* held great power and control over the *phrai*, who had to obey every command of the *nai* under threat of state-sanctioned punishment.

Sakdina evolved into a complex hierarchical system of land ownership, hence the name *sakdina*, literally "power of the rice fields." The Thai king, with unlimited power, originally owned all of the land. In the fifteenth century, King Boroma Trailokkanat (CE 1448–1488) enacted the Law of the Civil Hierarchy, which classified and placed every individual, irrespective of land-holdings, in a number ranking system by assigning the person a certain numerical *sakdina*.

"In the exhaustive laws of King Trailokkanat's reign, every possible position and status was assigned a number, thus specifying everyone's relative position in an enormously complex hierarchy."

Eisenstadt and Roniger point out that the Thai king used the *sakdina* system to curtail the development of independent power domains. The king "attempted, more or less successfully, to retain the *nais'* allegiance by applying a complicated hierarchical system of awards of rank, honorific names and elaborate "dignity" (*sakdina*) which extended from the highest official to the meanest landowner." The great majority of the Siamese population, known as *phrai* or commoners, held a *sakdina* rank of between 10 and 350.

Thais themselves classified every person as a member of four classes: royalty (*chao*), nobility (*khunang*), commoners (*phrai*), and slaves (*tat*).

The *sakdina* system was only one way of ranking Thais. In the seventeenth century, all commoners had to serve the king for six months of the year, an onerous service known as corvee. The king appointed government administrators to supervise this service by assigning a number of commoners to each administrator. The commoners or *phrai* assigned to work under an administrator called their supervisor *nai*, meaning master or patron,

The *nai* had complete control over the services of each *phrai* for whom he was responsible. On the other hand, the *phrai* expected provision and protection. Social scientists regard *nai-phrai* patronage as a significant historical root of the patron-client system. "The nature of the *prai* and *nai* relationship was that of client and patron . . . a relationship between two persons of superiority and inferiority."

Thais use the linguistic term *phii-nong* to express the values, which undergird the patron client system. *Phii-nong* is a dyadic Thai relationship designation that literally means older-younger, but more broadly refers to seniority. Thai people measure seniority in relation to power, wealth, professional rank, education, age, merit, and birth. Deference is normally given to each of these domains of seniority, and the moral obligation for senior people to care for juniors is universally recognized. Almost all Thai people refer to each other as *phii* or *nong*, and the assumption is that the more senior will guard the welfare of the younger whenever and wherever necessary. The importance of this system is apparent from the relative absence of surnames in Thailand. Almost all Thai people, from the youngest kindergarten child to the Prime Minister, are known by their first name, preceded by a *phii-nong* title, rather than their surname. Historically, surnames did not even exist for commoners until 1916. Today, Thai people continue to use relationship terminology that indicates their relative status such as *phii* or *nong* rather than names or nicknames to refer to themselves or the other in all interactions. The moral duties and privileges of the relationship roles are inherent to the relationship titles.

The nature of the patron-client system has changed and developed over time. After Thailand opened its borders to international trade during the mid-nineteenth century, the socio-economic changes in society caused patron-client relationship ties to evolve into informal network ties, or "circles."

Relationships within the circles became more diffuse and uncertain so that both client and patron could only hope and trust that each side would fulfill their expectations. These older structures have changed to such a degree that the observer can find hardly any trace of them in present-day society. By contrast, the informal rules governing proper behavior in personal relationships continue to exist within families and social structures even today. Informal rules behind the structures continue to guide many of the social interactions between older relatives and children, the king and his subjects as well as the relations between senior public servants and their juniors.

A somewhat surprising characteristic of current Thai clientism is the lack of personal commitment to their patrons. In an uncertain environment, clients have not hesitated to change their allegiance whenever their patrons were unwilling or unable to provide resources to them. Alan Johnson proposes that this lack of personal commitment shows that rather than ascribing a strict patron-client rubric to Thai social relationships, researchers should describe them as inherently hierarchical.

The Legacy of the Patron-client System

These intrinsic hierarchist values continue to wield a powerful influence on the social relationships between mission partners in Thailand. Every relationship between Thai and expatriate mission partners has some power inequality. Expatriate team leaders have commented that their Thai team members always want money and are never satisfied. Thais have accused their expatriate leaders of being "stingy and uncaring." These observations show that Christian mission partners perhaps unwittingly continue to play out patron-client roles.

Suntaree Komin's study of Thai values highlights the significance of obligation in the Thai social system. Komin ranks the "grateful relationship orientation" (*bunkhun*) second out of nine value clusters in terms of its order of importance to Thai people. *Bunkhun* describes a relationship where each party is aware of feelings of indebtedness and gratitude. Taylor also observed that *bunkhun* is a strong value underlying the hierarchical nature of Thai society: "There is no English equivalent of the term *bunkhun*, but it may be described as any good thing, help or favor done by someone which entails gratitude and obligation on the part of the beneficiary."[1]

This obligation between two parties is the underlying value that gives rise to the patron-client bond in Thailand. The patron gives favors to the client, setting up an indebted relationship. Patron-client ties are psychologically binding long-term obligations based on favors and benefits obtained by each party within the relationship. Being constantly aware and conscious of the *bunkhun* debt they must repay is a highly valued character trait known as *katanyu* (gratitude).

Akin Rabibhadana described an important dichotomy in Thai life between *sung* (high) and *tam* (low) where patron-client values control behavior.

One of the first things a Thai child learns is the distinction between high and low (*ruchak thi sung thi tam*). In social relations, the distinction is between *phuyai* (superior) and *phunoi* (inferior). The behaviors that the phunoi must exhibit towards the phuyai are *khaorop* (respect), *chueafang* (obedience) and *krengjai* (fear of doing anything that would offend another).

Steve Taylor found that the patron-client social structure has influenced the Christian beliefs of Thai church leaders and members. Taylor's research suggests that Thai Christians tend to see God as a great patron. The same Thai word, *phrachao*, is used for God, Buddha, and the king. The king is the most wonderful patron in the eyes of the Thai people. Taylor said that Thai Christians regard God as "a holy, powerful, benevolent Lord. He is the ideal patron spirit and king. His power is unlimited, and his love and benevolence is very great to those who respect and obey him."

However, Taylor and Hughes both found that Thai Christians often do not feel a deep sense of indebtedness to God, and that the Thais' relationship with God is transactional.

---

1. Taylor, "Gaps in Beliefs," 79.

Devoted to Christ

When God blesses them materially or with good health, they return the favor by gratitude and loyalty, expressed through church attendance and prayer. However, when they feel God does not bless them, there is the temptation to look for another patron, or doubt whether God is truly powerful.

How Thai Leaders Exercise Power

The legacy of the patron-client system in Thailand has given rise to a sharp dichotomy between those of high rank who have power and those of inferior status who do not. Thailand's leaders are its political elite, composed of its bureaucratic staff and decision-making heads and 10–15 grand policy-makers. The decision-making elite comprises retired generals and top military personnel whose power is so great that the Thai parliament and prime minister all defer to their instructions. Military personnel have always been seen as men of authority. During the times of absolute monarchy, kings depended on the strength of the military to keep them in power, so that in essence, the military had ultimate decision-making power.

There is a strong moral dimension to leadership in Thailand. Thai people firmly believe that leaders have both the legitimacy and the moral right to hold decision-making power, or otherwise they would not be able to remain in their position. Conversely, followers have the moral duty to accept leaders and their decisions. These values and beliefs continue to influence Thai people's ideas about leadership, even in the church and other Christian institutions. The moral component of leadership shines out from the word that is used by Thais to refer to the patron client system as it functions in Thailand. This word is *rabob-ooppathum*, a term that literally means "system of moral care." When Thais have been asked what they understood by this term their responses had a positive moral component: for example, "It means an older person taking care of a younger person"; "to look after someone, to support them"; "to be kind"; and "being a righteous person to those who need your help."

Those at the top of this power structure are able to hold onto their power because they are assumed to have the legitimate moral right of leadership. Thais argue that if the leader did not have this right. The leader would not remain long in this position. Hence, in Thailand a follower has the moral duty to accept both the leader and his decisions.

Where Is My Patron?

Thai team members have sometimes regarded missionaries as high-status patrons with the obligation to provide for followers. A tragic, true story illustrates this well. After Peter came from America to start a gospel radio ministry in Bangkok, a young man named Jamlong was soon converted through listening to the broadcasts. Jamlong joined Peter's team, helping him to follow up thousands of Buddhist people who responded to the radio messages. After five years, Peter turned the leadership of his ministry over to Jamlong, and moved with his family to California. That same year Peter's mission organization bought a building to house a radio studio and registered it in Jamlong's name to serve as a base for continued ministry.

Ten years later, a serious breakdown in trust and communication resulted between the mission organization and the local ministry in Thailand. While the International Director Bob was on a scheduled visit to Thailand, Jamlong's father unexpectedly died. Because of his Christian faith, Jamlong was not willing to take his father to the local Buddhist temple for cremation. He thanked God for the timing of Bob's visit, clearly expecting him to pay for a Christian funeral and burial. Nevertheless, Bob made no effort to discuss Jamlong's financial situation with him, and he did not contribute towards funeral expenses. In fact, Bob was extremely uncomfortable, and after a short prayer, left as quickly as possible. Jamlong was hurt and offended. He mentioned to a Thai Christian leader how he would never forget the day he met Bob. His heart was deeply grieving as his father had died two days earlier and Jamlong had no money. What could he do? He thought that if he were still a Buddhist he would have taken his body to the temple immediately. But he was now a Christian and wanted a Christian funeral for his father. Unfortunately, such cost quite a lot of money. He had been working hard for Peter and Bob's organization a long time and assumed Bob should look after Jamlong and his family. Yet, instead of generous, he ended up, in his own account, viewing Bob as horrible, mean and stingy. Bob simply stared at his father's body and left right away. As Jamlong noted, Bob had as much compassion on his father as people would have on a dead dog.

Bob's failure to fulfill cultural expectations had grave consequences. Within a few months, Jamlong had severed his connection with all Christian churches and organizations. He sold the building that had housed the radio studio to pay his debts and provide funds to look after the future needs of his family. The radio ministry ceased, and the mission leaders have not been able to contact Jamlong. There are reports that he was broken-hearted, and eventually left the Christian faith.

There was an obvious and a deep disparity between the Western values of Peter, Bob, and the mission leaders, and the cultural values held by Jamlong and his Thai team. Peter and his family had come to Thailand, professing that they did not need a salary because God took care of them and met their needs. Consequently, when they left Thailand and appointed Jamlong into a leadership role, they made very little provision for him to receive an adequate salary. Medical care and other social security benefits were nonexistent. The missionaries from America had a large supporter base, and any time they had a financial need, they wrote letters to their supporters and the funds were quickly provided. Jamlong, on the other hand, was converted from Buddhism, and virtually disinherited from his family for what they considered treacherous behavior. The Christian population 40 years ago was even smaller then than it is today, so that any appeals for funds Jamlong made were ignored. The fact that he had aligned himself with rich foreigners meant that to his family he was regarded as a source of funds rather than a person in need of their assistance.

Jamlong, a recent convert, naturally believed that he was in a reciprocal relationship of obligation with Peter and Bob, expecting them to behave as patrons who would show beneficence and generous support. When they did not, he became very bitter. He called them heartless, stingy, and ungrateful for the sacrifices he had made. In fact, Jamlong was a diligent, meticulous, responsible leader who tried his best to carry out Peter's instructions. From his cultural perspective, he fulfilled his duty as a good client, but felt completely abandoned when his patrons did not fulfill their obligations. On the other hand, Bob was shocked when he heard of Jamlong's reaction to his visit. He said, "If he wanted money, why didn't he say so? He smiled at me and was very friendly. How was I supposed to know if he didn't tell me?" This is an extreme example where ignorance of cultural values led to the catastrophic obliteration of ministry vision and goal implementation.

How then should expatriate missionaries work with their Thai partners? How should they exercise leadership?

Understand and Adjust to the Thai leadership style

Leadership does not happen in a vacuum, but in a social and religious context where people's cultural values lead them to think very differently from expatriate mission partners. Effective mission leadership means understanding the cultural rules by which leaders govern. In Thailand, the default cultural expectation for team leaders is the same as that for Thai patrons. They should be respectable, be worthy of honor and have authority while at the same time they must be benevolent, provide protection, emotional support, favors, cover the mistakes of his subordinates, and reward them lavishly. Through the patron's many acts of kindness, the client's indebtedness is built up. The client in turn must show deference, giving the patron honor, respect, loyalty, and trust. Thais expect their ideal leader to exercise a combination of authority and benevolence. This gives a leader *baramee*, or power that comes from the respect and loyalty of followers. The whole basis of the *rabob-ooppathum* patron-client system is a moral obligation to exercise power in a benevolent way. This implies that Thais expect leaders to exhibit a blend of authoritarianism (but not despotism) and benevolence towards their followers. The two strands woven into the leader's mantle are called *phradet* (authority) and *phrakhun* (benevolent patronage). A leader who finds the right balance between these two factors has *baramee*—power and strength derived from respect and loyalty.

Mission leaders working in patron-client cultures would do well to reframe their world so they can follow Biblical principles more closely. Lingenfelter characterized the incarnation of Jesus Christ as the only reliable model of mission work and ministry.[2] Jesus was fully God and yet he lived a fully human life within the world of Jewish culture. Missionaries who follow Jesus' example in seeking to incarnate into a new culture will necessarily experience the stress of drastic personal and social reorientation. It is very stressful for mission partners from egalitarian cultures to find themselves regarded as high-status patrons with an obligation to provide for their followers. But in fact, the Bible speaks to all cultures and challenges all values. The only absolute cultural values that Christian believers must adopt are the Biblical values exemplified in the life of Jesus.

Create Partnerships of Interdependence

The simplest definition of partnership is "using mutual gifts to accomplish tasks." True partnership means that the contribution of every member of the team is equally valuable. While the patron-client system is based on unequal power relations, the Christian perspective is that all mission partners,

2. Lingenfelter, *Ministering Cross-Culturally*, 14–19.

no matter what their cultural, national, or socio-economic background, have equally valuable gifts to contribute to accomplish the team task. While some partners might bring more resources than others, effective partnership means that each one contributes equally valuable but differing gifts and abilities to the partnership. Bob and Peter, for example, brought vision and finances to the radio work, but Jamlong had language skills, cultural knowledge, social contacts and commitment that greatly enriched the ministry.

Jamlong's world-view was strongly influenced by traditional patron-client values, while Peter and Bob were from an egalitarian society. Failure to understand their responsibilities according to Thai cultural values led to a tragic relationship and team breakdown. A deep value dissonance between the hierarchist, collective values held by Jamlong and the more egalitarian, individualist values of Peter and Bob led to the dissolution of the team and the collapse of the whole ministry.

If Peter and Bob had taken seriously their responsibility to understand Jamlong's worldview, and humbly studied God's word together with Jamlong, the outcome could have been very different. One of the fundamental obligations that Peter, the team leader, and Bob the International Director failed to meet was to provide financially for Jamlong's family, particularly following the death of his father. Jamlong, a relatively recent convert from Buddhism, regarded Peter and Bob as patrons, morally obligated to take care of his financial needs as long as he fulfilled his role as a client by meticulously obeying their orders. He was deeply shocked when they failed to take care of his financial needs in a time of family crisis. But who should have been Jamlong's provider? He was a new believer, a child of God. Every believer is dependent upon God's provision for daily needs. Peter and Bob missed their opportunity to sit down with Jamlong and humbly study together what God's word says about money, financial responsibility and financial provision. God not only dispenses benefactions upon all people (Acts 14:17) but also becomes a personal patron to believers who receive his son. They become part of God's family and enjoy special access to divine favors.

Perhaps Bob and Peter should have seen their own need to repent from an unhealthy reliance on financial supporters rather than on their heavenly Provider.

Scripture clearly teaches that God owns everything, so the Western church does not own all the resources for the task of mission. Rather than have the mind-set that Christian leaders should maintain independence or create dependence, the whole church of Jesus Christ needs to move towards a healthy interdependence. Paul Rajkumar Gupta writes, "Unless we come to realize that everything is from God, everything belongs to God and unless we learn to be better stewards, we will continue to have the dichotomy between the rich and the poor, the haves and the have-nots, the developed and the underdeveloped, the east and the west."

While the scriptures teach that money is a blessing from God that Christians should use wisely, the Bible also warns that money has the potential to be worshipped as mammon, a rival god that people depend on and worship in place of God. In common Thai thought, though, wealth or poverty is viewed as the result of one's karma, or the amount of merit accumulated in previous incarnations. Many Thai believers still see the rich as morally superior to people below them on the socio-economic scale. Thai and expatriate mission partners in Thailand must actively and intentionally search the scriptures so that together they can challenge cultural beliefs regarding money that oppose scriptural teaching.

Certain Thai cultural values that are based on karma and the patron-client system are out of harmony with the scriptural depiction of money. Thai leaders often feel pressure to access sources of money that they could use to validate themselves as patrons to those below them in the hierarchy. The heritage of the patron-client system has caused Thai leaders to feel continually obligated to provide financial resources for their followers. Young Thai leaders sometimes resist the call to leadership, because they feel unable to meet the financial obligations to provide for followers. Mission organizations need to understand and acknowledge the pressure of patron-client obligations on Thai leaders, and sensitively help them to adequately deal with economic issues. If they do not, the unequal power relations surrounding money and resources will inhibit goal fulfilment and team effectiveness.

With increasing modernization and development in Thailand, traditional patron-client relationships have eroded, and consequently only form one dimension of Thai social relations, which have complexified significantly. At the same time, hierarchical relationships still exist where Thais and expatriate mission partners work together in Thailand. This should come as no surprise, for "centuries of intense social rigidity are not easy to reform, and the ghost of *sakdi na* continues to influence everyday Thai social relationships."

How then should mission partners in Thailand lead their teams? While Lingenfelter regards some leadership structures as superior (in the same way that kingship was more effective than the judgeship system in Israel), he suggests that the leadership style is less important than the leader's relationship with God.

Lingenfelter advised leaders to take the Biblical role of a pilgrim who allows scripture to challenge and transform leadership styles rather than unquestioningly following cultural norms and values.

Thai and expatriate mission leaders must reject the authoritarianism that lies at the center of the Thai power structure. On the other hand, the Thai ideal of benevolent leadership resonates with Jesus' teaching on servanthood, where leaders serve rather than exercise power to oppress their followers. This then opens the way for mission leaders in Thailand to use power to sensitively and humbly serve and minister to the needs of followers. Even in the most hierarchical environment, Thai and expatriate mission leaders can learn to use power creatively so that their relationships become a powerful testimony rather than a hindrance to the gospel message.

9

The Essence of Leadership
Mission From a Position of Weakness

PAUL YONGGAP JEONG

Introduction

Although I have seen and read many books on leadership, few discuss this topic from the perspective of the Kingdom of God. This is especially so in ways which require readers to think about leadership critically through the lens of a theology of the Kingdom of God. Even those that do discuss leadership and the Kingdom of God do so with such a broad and opaque definition of kingdom that such would have little practical impact on the exercise of leadership.

It is my contention here, however, that we must relate the Kingdom of God with the Suffering Servant of Yahweh, knowing that this Suffering Servant has brought the Reign of God in his person and ministry into the world. Doing so will significantly impact our understanding of leadership and may require much more caution. Apart from the clear understanding of the leadership style of Jesus, who identifies with the Isaianic suffering servant, a biblical understanding of leadership is not possible.

Among the various biblical scholars who discuss the Kingdom of God, I here focus on the work of John Bright in his book *The Kingdom of God*. According to Bright, in the Hebrew Bible there appears a tension between the Kingdom of God and the Davidic kingdom. That is, the various attempts to identify the Davidic kingdom with the Kingdom of God is rejected.

It was not the first time in the history of Israel that the Kingdom of God was to be distinguished from any human kingdom. Similar related tensions include Gideon's refusal to be king over the Israelites (Judg 8:22–23)

and the Prophet Samuel's negative response when the Israelites made a request to appoint a king to lead them (1 Sam 8:4–7).

It is the testimony of the New Testament that Israel's hope of a coming kingdom was fulfilled through the coming of the Suffering Servant of Yahweh. With Jesus' appearance, the character of the Kingdom, different that what had been expected, was fully revealed. This character of weakness and suffering is often lost on much modern leadership theory, which has frequently developed its notion of leadership more in terms of power, ability, accomplishment, and effectiveness, rather than suffering and weakness. I seldom see in the literature of leadership any discussion of "weakness." Yet, the Bible consistently emphasizes the aspect of "weakness" in the lives of great leaders. Such is evident in the life of the Apostle Paul (who is often called "the Apostle of weakness"), as I shall discuss in detail. Therefore, I present the thesis that in this "new era" that has come through the person and ministry of Jesus the Messiah, the core value of leadership should be founded upon the notion of "mission from a position of weakness." I have elaborated on this theme in my book, *Mission from a Position of Weakness*.

Because I truly believe that this same theme should be the firm basis for addressing the conception of leadership in a new way, I will proceed to address the issue using the issues I raise in my book.

What Is "Mission from a Position of Weakness"?

Mission from a position of weakness takes as primary Jesus' mission on the cross. Because Jesus' mission for the Kingdom of God was ultimately accomplished from a position of weakness on the cross, his church as it follows in mission should also proceed in missional activity and leadership from that same position of weakness.

In this new era ushered into history through the coming of the Kingdom in the person and ministry of Jesus Christ, the weakness of the cross was revealed as the hidden character of God's glorious Kingdom. The weakness of the cross actually turned out to be the living power of God, a power that exposed and disarmed the powers of darkness. This weakness must accompany the Church in her ministry.

"Mission from a position of weakness" is an approach that does not simply assume being weak for its own sake. Neither does it mean having a weak mission, nor a fruitless ministry. Since God, in this new era, has established the weakness of the cross as His way of demonstrating might and power, therefore the Church of Christ must understand that a position of weakness in faithfulness is mighty and humility is powerful. The people of God must recognize that God uses his church in all its vulnerability to demonstrate his power in revealing the true character of the gospel of God's Kingdom.

The Importance of This Topic

The importance of the issue of mission from a position of weakness becomes clear when we understand more fully the underlying meaning of the Kingdom of God. The key to understanding the essential meaning of the Kingdom rests on the self-sacrificial crucifixion of Christ. The cross is the focal point of God's Kingdom. If we fail to understand the crucifixion and its weakness as the center of the Kingdom, then we would miss the very essence of God's revelation, the revelation that the reign of God has come through the person and ministry of Jesus Christ, especially through the Messiah's sacrificial crucifixion.

Based on this point of view, much contemporary understanding of mission must be thoroughly reexamined. True mission must be measured from the perspective of God's Kingdom, because mission originates from that Kingdom. Mission exists for the Kingdom and it needs to be carried out through that perspective.

In this way, Jesus' model of mission becomes ours. Jesus initiated and completed his mission solely for the sake of the Kingdom of God. His mission was from a position of weakness. Therefore, the Church should carry out her mission in like manner, and so this mission must be done from the position of weakness.

This topic is of critical importance for the church today precisely because it was the manner by which Jesus carried out God's mission.

Devoted to Christ

The Method of the Presentation

Here, I would like to present the theme of mission from weakness in the New Testament by examining briefly Luke-Acts, and I & II Corinthians.

Mission From a Position of Weakness in Luke

The theme of mission from weakness runs through the entirety of Luke-Acts. The Gospel of Luke is known for dealing with the poor and those on the margins. The book of Acts is consistent with the Gospel of Luke in dealing with the theme of mission from weakness.

The Magnificat as a Model

As I note in my book, it is truly exceptional that the song of a plain young girl "overshadows the mood of the entire content of the Gospel of Luke in terms of reversal of status."

The song of a young girl, not a sophisticated statement by a great theologian, holds the key for understanding the reversal of status that takes place in the world through the coming of the Kingdom in Christ Jesus.

Mary's song begins with the expression of her personal experience, praising God for what he has done for her. This personal expression of her experience is "then gradually enlarged theologically, in singing an inspirational song with her lips, to the scope of the general reversal in the whole of human life."

Therefore, the song becomes a proclamation "that, through the Messiah whom she is to bear, the reversal will take place in every area of human society."

Repetition and contrast appear in the song: "'The humble state of his servant' (1:48) and 'the Mighty One' (1:49); 'scattered . . . proud' (1:51); 'brought down rulers' and 'lifted up the humble' (1:52); 'filled the hungry with good things' and 'sent the rich away empty' (1:53)."

By these examples, Luke emphasizes reversal.

It is in the personal experience of Mary that the almighty God meets the poor girl, lifts her up, and uses her to do his great things. Mary herself becomes God's instrument and serves as a model for doing mission from a position of weakness.

Elements of Mission from a Position of Weakness

The theme of contrast between the rich and the poor is strong in Luke and runs throughout his gospel.

The meaning of the poor in Luke concerns "the real have-nots of the world, who know an empty stomach," a contras to the usage in the Gospel of Matthew. Luke does not spiritualize the meaning of "the poor." Rather, for Luke, poor simply refers to those who experience economic lack. It is to such that Jesus says, "Blessed are you who are poor, for yours is the Kingdom of God" (6:20–26). Jesus strongly warns the rich, saying, "But woe to you who are rich, for you have already received your comfort" (6:24). In these few verses, Jesus intends to say that by giving the Kingdom to the poor "the God of Justice is leveling the gap between the rich and the poor."

Now, anyone who wants to enter the Kingdom should share it with the poor because the Kingdom belongs to the poor. What he seems to mean is not that the Kingdom is given to the poor because they are more righteous or because they deserve it. It is given because they are underprivileged and hopeless in this world and so turn to the Lord, the Gospel, and the coming Kingdom. As for the rich, they also can share the Kingdom with the poor as they give out to the poor whatever they have.

Luke also deals specifically with the issue of women. Among the earliest followers of Jesus was a group of women who came from Galilee (8:1–3). These women had followed Jesus from Galilee to Jerusalem and even to the place of his death. In the time of Jesus, Rabbis did not receive women disciples. It was not conceivable for a Rabbi to be accompanied by women. By allowing women among his close companions and immediate community of followers, Jesus was removing a significant cultural barrier and creating a new type of community in which a new quality of fellowship would be experienced.

These women from Galilee would be the ones who were at the cross until the last, and were first at the tomb where the risen Jesus had been.

Their role as a serving group at every critical point for Jesus was crucial and contrasting to the one of Jesus' male disciples. The service that they rendered to Jesus' band and their low status in the culture of Jesus' time qualifies their mission as one from a position of weakness.

One more story that contrasts this dynamic of female discipleship is the story of the sinful woman in 7:36–50. Luke uses this woman as a foil to Simon the Pharisee. This sinner is a female. Simon, a male, is a Pharisee, the cultural ideal of a righteous religious leader.

This woman lived on the margins of society and was not an invited guest to this party that Simon was hosting for Jesus. The woman was standing on the periphery, behind Jesus. Simon was at the very center of the scene, sitting with Jesus. The responses of both the woman and Simon toward Jesus were radically different. The "woman wept . . . wiping the tears with her hair, kissing his feet and pouring perfume on them" (7:38). Simon, by his inner musings of critique and judgment, was creating a psychological distance from Jesus.

The woman's lavish offering of the expensive perfume and her moving expression of affection toward Jesus is contrasts with Simon's coldness and indifference. In this sense, the woman's action is modeling the very service of the women disciples that appears in the next passage (8:2–3).

Jesus, as the Forgiver, not only forgives her sin, but also "uses her as a corrective to the religious leadership."

A third example of mission from weakness consists of the frequent appearance of widows in the Gospel of Luke.

Women in general were disadvantaged in that male-dominant society. Yet, among women, widows were the least protected and most vulnerable of all. In the time of Luke, every woman was to be under the protection of a male. They were to be mothers, wives, or sisters. If not, they were regarded as deprived of female honor. Additionally, they usually found themselves poor because they did not have husbands who could financially support them.

In two sequential passages (20:45–47 and 21:1–4), Luke highlights widows. First, in 20:45–47, the teachers of the law were warned by Jesus against their evil conduct. They enjoyed their religious influence and loved to be respected. They exploited widows by using false religious piety. They unethically received money from the widows while giving legal assistance to them. Their religious evil consisted of feigning devotion to attain the people's trust through the praying of long public prayers. Jesus announced that God's harshest condemnation would be upon them.

In the next passage (21:1–4), Luke makes a sharp contrast between the rich and the poor widow. Although the rich must have given more money than the poor, Jesus saw more than total contributions. The poor widow had given all she possessed.

In these two passages, Luke seems to be making the point that while the teachers of the law misuse their religious influence, the poor widow who could be among the ones exploited by the leaders is faithfully following the godly instruction that was taught by these teachers of the law. In this case, these widows become a foil to the religious leaders.

A fourth example of mission from a position of weakness consists of the children who appear in Luke as agents of mission from a position of weakness (9:1–50; 10:21–24; 18:15–17). These become "the powerful symbol for the greatness, the leadership, or the qualification for entry into the Kingdom of God, or the appropriate recipients of God's revelation."

In 9:46–48, the disciples begin to argue over who would be the greatest. Jesus, knowing their thoughts, has a child stand before them and says that whoever welcomes this child in his name welcomes him, and whoever welcomes him welcomes him who sent him. By saying this, Jesus surely means that the one humble enough to see the full authority of the presence of the Son and the One who sent the Son in a little child is a great person. This statement also implies that "the child is as important as a missionary who is sent in Jesus' name" (10:16).

While their master, Jesus, identified with the lowly and would eventually die for them on the cross, these disciples, who are to resemble their master, were arguing in a worldly manner over who would be the greatest. That is why in the preceding verses, in 9:43–45, "they failed to understand the Son of Man's suffering and were afraid to ask about it."

There are other elements relating to the theme of mission from weakness in Luke's gospel. Such exists, for example, in the dinner talk (14:7–11, 12–14, 15–24; 22:24–30) and in the stories about the tax collectors and sinners (5:27–32; 7:31–35; 15:1–32; 19:1–10).

Mission from a Position of Weakness in Acts

The most significant change that takes place in Acts in terms of mission from a position of weakness is relative to the disciples' understanding of *diakonia*. Yet, many readers of Acts likely fail to notice the significance of that central issue. Prior to the disciples' witness of the resurrected Jesus, their actual experience of watching their teacher being crucified was one of great confusion, uncertainty, and fear. Afterwards, as they witnessed Jesus' resurrection, they were filled with amazement and overjoyed. In the same instance, their memory flashed back to the brutality of his actual crucifixion on the cross. Their vivid memory of Jesus in great pain and suffering on the cross was still with them.

After they encountered the newly resurrected Jesus, they not only professed Jesus as the Son of God in an authentic way, but also began to fathom why their Lord had to suffer. That must have been the decisive moment in which they began to grapple with the significance of *diaconia*.

Earlier, the disciples were not able to grasp Jesus' teaching on servantship. In Luke 22:24–32, Jesus was celebrating the last Passover meal with his disciples. In this setting, the disciples were disputing who among them would be the greatest while at the very time their Lord was facing his imminent death. Their rivalry shown here was demonstrating the fact that the disciples were not able to understand the impending suffering of their Lord. The same kind of association between these two aspects also appears in Luke 9:44–48.

In Acts, however, the disciples' attitude changes. As they gathered after Jesus' ascension, the disciples officially express that they were called by God for *diakonia*. Peter in his address and prayer (Acts 1:17, 25) ensures that the disciples' calling for the diaconate is no less than their apostleship. In his prayer in 1:25, Peter places the diaconate before the apostleship, making sure that every ministry that they launch is based on their call for the diaconate. Their understanding and attitude had at last changed. It took place even before they received the Holy Spirit at Pentecost. This very notable transformation took place in Acts. From that point on, the theme of mission from a position of weakness in Acts is expressed through *diakonia*.

Although it does not seem that the Apostles knew how the history of the church and mission would unfold, or what would happen in the course of mission in terms of the details, they nevertheless acted according to the principle expressed in their confession; their primary calling is foremost to the diaconate. A critical circumstance in which they were to apply their call to the diaconate was to take care of the widows in their community. Out of this act, in the history of the early church, came the unexpected development of the serial events that shaped a drastic course.

In a situation in which they could not effectively perform both the duties of prayer and preaching and the care of needy widows, the apostles arranged a plan. They acknowledged the necessity that there should be two kinds of leadership functions for two kinds of *diakonia*; the first group is to be for the service (*diakonia*) of the word, and the second is to serve (*diakonize*) tables. This arrangement resulted in unexpected consequences.

The historical development thus far is interesting. Care for the widows was developed into selection of seven for diakonia on tables, which in turn led to Stephen's martyrdom, then to persecution, to the scattering of the believers, to anonymous believers' commitment to evangelism, and to evangelization of marginal people (the Greeks). At last, Antioch becomes the main base for the Gentile mission. Here Paul, the main figure in Acts, emerges as a servant-leader. The prophecy of Jesus in 1:8 is also most visibly fulfilled here. What I emphasize here is that seemingly unimportant elements such as care for the widows or selection of men of diakonia were the main causes for important events that unfold in Acts. Truly, the principle of mission from weakness strongly underlies the Christian movement from the beginning.

In summary, *diakonia* becomes in the book of Acts the backbone of the development of the Christian movement. The cross of Jesus, due to the disciples' memory and understanding, became the permanent foundation of their ministry. And their ministry, as it was literally expressing itself (ministry means service), was based upon their sense of calling to *diakonia* by their crucified Lord.

Mission From a Position of Weakness in 1 & 2 Corinthians

The cross of Christ is central in Paul's theology and ministry. It is such an overriding element in his life and ministry that he is often called the theologian of the cross. In his identification with Jesus Christ who completed his mission on the cross, Paul came to realize that the aspect of weakness inherent in the cross is crucial. His ministry is distinguished as one coming from weakness itself. In this respect, he is even called the apostle of weakness.

The contexts of 1 and 2 Corinthians are different from each other yet both address the same Corinthian community. In this church, there had been tension over different understandings between Paul and the congregation of what constituted the Christian gospel. In his effort to bring the Corinthians back to himself, Paul, who had planted the Corinthian church, validates both himself and the gospel he preached by constantly presenting the aspect of mission from a position of weakness. Throughout 1 and 2 Corinthians, Paul does this both by explicating the gospel message and the life of the gospel bearer in terms of weakness.

In 1 Corinthians, Paul sets the weakness of the cross, of the messenger (Paul himself), and of the Corinthians as the norm in the proclamation of the Gospel of the Kingdom (1 Cor 1:18—2:5). Paul's emphasis on weakness is repeated throughout 2 Corinthians. He speaks of comfort through suffering (1:3–5), glory through shame (2:14–4:6), life through death (4:7–15), and riches through poverty (8:1–15).

The theme of weakness reaches a crescendo in 2 Corinthians 12:1–10, with the theme of 'power made perfect through weakness.' From the first chapter of 1 Corinthians, Paul struggles in conflict with the Corinthians concerning the character of his apostleship and the gospel message. In saying that he received the truth about weakness from God himself (12:9), he claims authority for the character of the gospel that he proclaims, and also confirms that he is an apostle of weakness, not of power. There is a different kind of power at work in him, the power of the cross. Though from a human perspective it looks weak, this weakness is the guarantee that the gospel that Paul preaches is genuine. For the sake of the Christ who was crucified, he had become weak.

We know from 2 Corinthians that Paul succeeded in his defense of his gospel for which the weakness of the cross is foundational. By doing so, his effort to bring back the Corinthians to himself succeeded. With consistency in both 1 and 2 Corinthians, Paul vehemently defends his mission as one from a position of weakness.

Conclusion

Mission from a position of weakness is not a new concept. Not only does it appear in the New Testament, but it is also present in theological and missiological literature. However, because of an overarching recent trend of the application of "power" to mission in order to reach a certain goal, the reality that God's power is manifested in weakness has been buried in more recent missiological conversations and missional practice. It seems that the most important treasure in our mission thinking has been significantly obscured, at times even completely lost. There have been prominent missiologists and theologians who have addressed the importance of this theme in mission. Lesslie Newbigin originally used the phrase "mission from a position of weakness" in his book, *The Open Secret*, and elucidated this idea in other writings.[1] David Bosch, in his last speech, spoke on vulnerability.[2] Jürgen Moltmann (on the theology of the cross), John Howard

1. See Newbigin, *Open Secret*, 5.
2. See Bosch, *Vulnerability of Mission*.

Yoder, and Jacob Loewen (on self-exposure) are among those keenly aware of the importance of mission from weakness.

In the present mission context, a general trend is that the most powerful countries send the most missionaries. Along with their national power, inherently comes the power of money, information, tools, knowledge, personnel, etc. Using these resources, in themselves, is not wrong. These mission resources should be used as a means to reach goals in mission. However, the use of these resources will never guarantee true effectiveness in mission, nor genuine leadership development models. In actuality, if used uncritically and inappropriately, they may actually undercut the true goals of mission by impairing mission from weakness, unwittingly authorizing undesirable, non-biblical leadership models. Depending on how such resources are used, they can actually counter the authentic and long-lasting fruitfulness of mission.

The importance of this theme of mission from a position of weakness currently does not enjoy a prominent place in the missiological arena. Despite this obscurity today, the magnitude of this theme should be significant for future mission, future academic missiology, and future leadership development models. The correct understanding of mission from a position of weakness by missionaries, Christian workers, and missiologists is crucial for future generations. As God's people in mission willingly accept "weakness" that accompanies them because of their obedience to their God, the Almighty God will demonstrate his power through their weakness, power that is indescribable and immeasurable.

10

Practical and Missiological Implications for the Transformation of Machismo

WILMER VILLACORTA

I am indebted to Sherwood Lingenfelter for his valuable guidance and contributions for the following research. His ample understanding of social anthropology not only enriched my conclusions, but also furthered my thinking in the field. My heartfelt thanks, as always, go to Sherwood for his inspiration, mentoring, friendship, and challenging dialogue. I am deeply appreciative of his sharp mind and servant's heart.

Summary of the Study

This research represents an exploratory study on the complexity of machismo as a sociocultural construct. The structure of the study was designed through data collection, observation, inquiry, triangulation, analysis and interpretation of the interpersonal interactions and social relationships among Andean leaders in central Peru. The focus of the field research aims to describe the possible interactions of machismo in leadership practice in congregational context among six Pentecostal denominations.

In this study, I obtain original data on machismo that directly addresses its challenges on leaders and leadership practice. Machismo is often considered unique to Latin American culture. Additionally, it is frequently assumed as nonexistent in evangelical circles in Latin America. This study deals with how leaders in Andean Pentecostal churches confront the tension and complexities of this deeply rooted issue of control and power called machismo. In particular, appropriating the theoretical approach of women's research on machismo, I argue this study that varying degrees of machismo exist in the behaviors, attitudes and interactions of male pastors, and that these variations take place in the context of suffering in the lives of male pastors.

This essay provides a new perspective on discussions of machismo in the Latin context in at least two ways. First, I trace the roots that engender and the factors that shape machismo among Andean Pentecostal leaders. Second, in this study I suggest a process to manage machismo, enabling leaders to become more effective in a machismo-laden context. I address specific areas to instill within leaders transformed behaviors, attitudes and interactions in male/female and male/male relationships. In what follows, I suggest a transformational framework for machismo described through four significant processes: unmasking, identification, malleability and re-orientation. Furthermore, I discuss important missiological issues I draw out from implications of unmasking and malleability.

Transformational Framework

From my research, I identify four major themes that warrant careful attention: Faces of Machismo, Unmasking of Machismo, Malleability of Machismo, and Transforming Factors.

The underlying rationale for this fourfold framework I offer here relies on a constructivist view of machismo, which asserts that machismo is dynamic and susceptible to variations. Each of its elements interacts with leaders who undergo critical circumstances that allow this process to happen.

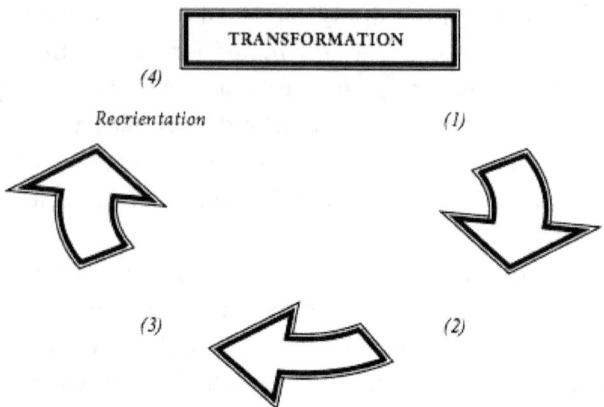

Figure 1. A Transformational Framework

This framework depicts a transformational process that takes place in the life of a male leader immersed in a machismo-laden context. Through the identification of the dichotomy in machismo, the unmasking and malleability of machismo along with its behaviors and interactions are reoriented from destructive to constructive patterns. These are:

Unmasking	Identifying and internalizing critical circumstances in life.
Identification	Recognizing the public and private issues in relationships and roles.
Malleability	Managing, adapting new patterns of behavior, attitudes and interactions.
Reorientation	Applying and establishing new dimensions of relationships and partnership in congregational life.

The confluence of these central elements results in transformation. Unleashing healthy gender relationships and mutual interdependence and effectiveness in congregational life become the most significant and restorative outcomes.

Unmasking As Suffering

This initial metaphor captures the machismo *persona* represented in the image of a mask. The research data suggests that any person (male or female) may hide behind this mask. Leaders who appear to exert control and who use power indiscriminately are experts in depending on this façade.

From my research, I concluded that machismo-laden leaders wear the mask of machismo to intimidate and subordinate females and males alike. They also wear this machismo mask for the purpose of gaining and displaying an image of authority. Thus, the mask embodies machismo dynamics such as controlling behaviors, obsessive dominance and superficiality.

Simply defined, unmasking disrupts this dependency on the mask and its effects on relationships and behaviors through critical circumstances in the lives of male pastors. The following terms bring different dimensions of suffering into the framework.

Disclosing

Disclosure here refers to the act of making known to others information that is personal and private. Leaders in this study shared difficult life experiences that resulted from machismo being inflicted upon them, their mothers or other women in their lives. The disclosing of information, experiences, feelings and crises produced pain in a number of males who participated in the interviews.[1] Leaders who had grown up alone as street children or as fatherless sons shared their pain through tears, silence and bitterness, revealing that suffering occurs as leaders disclose their inner life circumstances.

Pruning

Character transformation was indeed a major outcome of suffering in the lives of participants. Unmasking produced refinement in attitudes flowing from the heart; I define this refinement as "pruning." The idea of pruning suggests removal of essential parts to encourage growth and fruitfulness.[2] Data indicated that leaders who were confronted by the unmasking process were enabled to reassess coercive and dominating behaviors. The unmasking process illuminated the areas of character that relied upon the misuse of power in relationship with others.

---

1. Twenty-eight pastors who participated in this study.

2. Trebesch uses this metaphor to describe and illustrate the deep sense of loss and pain (see Trebesch, *Isolation*, 35–38).

Devoted to Christ

Disarming

The process of disarming through the experience of critical circumstances worked to disable the systems that contributed to coercive behavior. Suffering confronts machismo, stripping it of its power, rendering it helpless. The mask of flawed power and control was disrupted when confronted with pain and uncertainty. To put it simply, machismo loses its power through brokenness. Though it does not disappear, always waiting in the wings to reassert itself, a transformed and equipped leader—with adequate support—may find true freedom from its sway.

Identification

The second step in this framework is the process by which a leader navigates reentry to his private/domestic sphere of life. The research data revealed the importance of two categories in this process: (1) Marriage, and (2) Parental role. Three headings captured the responses of male leaders as they were confronted with their recovered roles in their families: Realization, Coming to Terms and Understanding.[3]

Submission for men is particularly difficult and antithetical to many men and their masculine gender role identity.[4] Undeniably, when male leaders return to the private/domestic sphere after experiencing critical circumstances, it becomes highly likely that they will enter into a process of submission. As they learn to identify what matters, they become more submissive to what God intends them to learn.

Malleability

Following the identification process, a male leader is more susceptible to changes in behaviors and interactions with. This malleability dynamic, along with unmasking, provides a robust opportunity for transformation of machismo. This does not mean that machismo is eliminated; rather, it

---

3. *Realization* describes acknowledging relationships within the home environment as significant, safe and nurturing. *Coming to Terms* means to appreciate the wife's role, to enjoy living at home, and to admit that the wife and children roles are important. *Understanding* explains assessment of relationship in marriage, grasp essential of parental relationships and admit influence of wife in his life.

4. Plumb-Takamoto, "Liminality."

becomes adaptable and manageable. In other words, leaders experiencing malleability can reorient their attitudes, behaviors and interactions for the better, freed from machismo cultural expectations. Malleability in domestic relations, in congregational relations, and in interpersonal relations represents a major finding from this data. The following headings capture the response of male leaders as they are confronted with needed changes in their lives: Adaptability, Managing Better, Freedom, and Restructuring.[5]

Malleability is essentially a changing dynamic. The analysis of concrete behaviors and interactions of leaders facing suffering has allowed us to see malleability and how it is played out in context by males and females.[6]

Reorientation

The reorientation process is the final step in the framework leading to transformation. Since the goal of transformation primarily relates to behaviors and interactions, variations are described in terms of patterns. I define these patterns as: (1) Patterns of flexibility and accessibility, (2) patterns of resourcefulness and generosity, (3) patterns of relationship and connectedness.

Flexibility and Accessibility

These suggest that male and female congregational members may engage together in collective/cooperative activities. Thus, machismo loses its force when unity, interdependence and role are exchanged dynamically in social relationships.

Resourcefulness and Generosity

The recovery of the female participation in congregational life contributes to a new partnership model. Male pastors are enabled to recognize females'

---

5. These headings illustrate transformed behaviors in leaders who learn to implement better ways of relating with others within their public and private sphere circles.

6. Although the focus of this study is on male pastors, I suspect that this transformational framework is also applicable to females. I do not intend to fully elaborate on it since it is beyond the scope of this research. Further research may be able to explore how females face brokenness as leaders.

activities and skills and learn new patterns of giving and challenging cultural expectations of independence.

Relationship and Connectedness

The patterns of relationship and connectedness revitalize male pastors' efforts through new relational dynamics.

Discussion and Summary

The framework is tentatively integrating the main themes emerging from the data as these relate to the possible interactions of machismo in leadership practice among Andean Pentecostal leaders. However, leaders must pay attention to the significance of suffering in the lives of practitioners in the congregations. Careful reflection on the issues of suffering will help lessen the stress and complexity of transformation.

Basic Rationale for Missiological Discussion

Samuel Escobar suggests that the relevance of missiology in the Latin American context should be deeply transformational, responding to the hope of creating a new humanity by the proclamation of the good news and social transformation.[7] I hope to expand the significance of this study of machismo and its implications for transformation in the practice of leadership among Andean Pentecostal congregations along the lines of Escobar's perspective of transformational missiology.

Missiological Implications

After dealing with the practical outcomes of the transformational framework, I summarize the most relevant missiological contributions of this research. These insights have converged because of the field research, contributing theoretical models, personal journey and ministry experience. They provide significant implications for missional engagement.

---

7. Escobar, "Pauline Paradigm of Mission."

Insights Illuminating the Discussion

First, machismo without social relationships is simply a noun. It primarily deals with the power and control dynamics that take place not only in male/female relationships but also in male/male interaction. These theoretical perspectives became more meaningful to me as I observed the collected data once I returned from the field.[8]

Second, machismo relationships are dynamic and as such are the *loci* for the struggle of power and control in human interaction. In the search for power over others, machismo behavior adapts to allow both males and females to seek alternative ways to relate with others.

We humans learn to express feelings, ideas and convictions in part through the games we play as children. Culture allows us to play games as part of the fabric of our social and interpersonal interactions.[9] Games have rules that affect the way any person (male or female) chooses to behave and display his or her attitudes and convictions. They allow both males and females to exercise control in their relationships and use of power.[10]

Third, leaders in the Andean Pentecostal context operate with a natural immersion in machismo culture. The fluidity of the construct (machismo) cannot be eliminated from its embedding culture. Pretending that one could rid oneself completely of machismo should is *naive*. Conversion does not undo the effect of machismo like a magic spell, though some tend to believe such, denying the continuing subtle and tacit power of machismo. Realistically, therefore, character transformation must not be defined in

---

8. I must confess to my strong biases when I first began my research. My perspectives on machismo assumed unjustified domination inflicted on us (Latin Americans) through the accounts of the Spanish conquest. In other words, I had a limited view on the origins of machismo (Tamez, *Against Machismo*). My definition of machismo was solely limited to historical facts without looking at the larger picture. In this study, machismo deals more with behaviors and attitudes in Christian leaders and not so much with the "myth of machismo" (Castañeda, *Machismo Invisible*) that states the sexual prowess and dysfunctions (Stevens and Pescatello, *Marianismo*).

9. Lingenfelter, *Agents of Transformation*.

10. Even when machismo seems domesticated (Brusco, *Reformation of Machismo*), my research data suggests that the changed behaviors may not necessarily lead to domestic abuse or an overtly double-standard lifestyle. Since these behaviors are restricted by religious convictions, as in the case of Andean Pentecostal leaders, these restrictions eventually are altered by new patterns of behaviors. So, where there was physical abuse prior to conversion, now it is modified as verbal abuse, which is subtly played in the private/domestic sphere of life. Thus, the cycle of machismo, though modified, continues pervasively.

terms of how well one uses malleability or how one lives an unmasked machismo free life. Being more like Christ (through spiritual disciplines and community) becomes a process of transformation in the midst of a machismo-laden context.

Fourth, the unmasking process of machismo does not necessarily result in free leaders. Leaders continue to be part of the cultural games but through unmasking. They find new freedom to manage machismo—playing the game, and adapting for transformational relationships. I have observed how male pastors, having undergone the unmasking process, are capable of using the mask in machismo contexts. However, they no longer depend on such; nor do they base their significance on it. It is in these circumstances that malleability exhibits.

Fifth, the metaphorical mask of machismo is used in this research to illustrate two important characteristics: (1) Machismo requires social relationships to affirm it, and (2) machismo is a hybrid or neutral concept.

Sixth, the malleability of machismo is so adaptable that it also impacts how females lead others. Thus, machismo also informs leadership practice among females, displayed in directive behaviors characterized by yelling, rigidity and dominance.

Lastly, leaders in a machismo-laden context, particularly in Andean Pentecostalism, cannot focus on the significant task of selecting and developing followers, as machismo hinders the leaders' ability to see continuity and growth, maintaining a cycle of dominance by one leader.

Missiological Reflection

The purpose of this reflection is twofold: (1) To provide perspective and direction to the interactions of leaders within machismo-laden context, and (2) to provide suggestions that respond to the challenge of leadership practice *vis-à-vis* machismo among Andean Pentecostal congregations.

This study considers that the topic is not uniformly translatable to every context. The multifaceted symbols of suffering contain deep cultural connotations. Though I do not pretend to elaborate exhaustively on each category emerging from the field research, I frame these research findings around some significant missiological motifs.

Based on these findings, it is possible to argue that transformation is a dynamic process in which suffering becomes a significant factor that both challenges and produces variations on machismo. Given this, I will elaborate on: (1) suffering as a means of transformation; (2) malleability as an element of renewal that maintains transformation and (3) the factors of malleability as a pathway to inclusiveness.

Suffering

The theological motifs in this study emerge from the central motif of suffering. The ultimate Christian symbol of the cross conveys the ideas of suffering, death to self and weakness. Throughout this study, suffering becomes catalytic as Andean Pentecostal leaders are confronted with critical circumstances in their personal lives and ministry context.

Unmasking: A Way of Suffering

The dysfunctions of the mask are distortions imposed on any person by the culture from which he/she emerges. Suffering unmasks and disarms the distorted images of the mask of machismo that erode relationships through the misuse of power and control. The sins of the mask include exclusion, rejection, coercion, abuse, obsessive control, superficiality and selfishness. Unmasking often occurs through painful life circumstances that disrupt the effect of sin in a leader's life, his/her relationships, and priorities.

In the case of leaders in machismo-laden contexts, suffering dismantles the distorted masks that directly affect their leadership practice, producing a deeper evaluation of what a life in relationship with others should be, an ongoing prioritization of what gives life its deepest significance.

Passage: The Unavoidable Reality

The process of passage is a transition from one significant stage of life into a new one.[11] A passage often requires the paradoxical movement Turner describes, where "for an individual to go higher on the status ladder, he [she] must go lower than the status ladder."[12] This process encompasses humiliation—the unavoidable reality leaders in machismo culture undergo in the process of transformation.

---

11. Plumb-Takamoto, "Liminality."
12. Turner, *Ritual Process*, 17.

This image of suffering as passage relates to the mystery of the incarnation, which conveys images of dependence, childlike disposition and vulnerability. Lingenfelter and Mayers[13] describe it as "undergoing drastic personal reorientation." Simply stated, a passage brings change and hope as demonstrated in the process of unmasking machismo.

Strength in Weakness: The Power of Acknowledged Weakness

The macho code imposes that "Thou shalt not cry or expose feeling of emotion, fear or sympathy."[14] Leaders live and operate under the restriction of machismo culture, wherein weakness is an unacceptable trait. Suffering, however, confronts and exposes true weakness, when the mask of machismo is removed and transformation, if embraced, takes place.

Admitting weakness opens a pathway to inclusiveness in relationship with God and others. The cry of the Pauline passage of transformation is found in the fact that "power is perfected in weakness" (2 Cor 12:9, NASB). Pastors and leaders are called to live in the tension where strength and weakness meet and interact.[15] Suffering in all its manifestations reduces human pride to humility; in Shuster's words, "suffering is the intent of the Creator."[16] The strength that comes from suffering and vulnerability produces changes in how a person relates to others. Mending and restoring relationships becomes significant.

Correct Use of Power: Spirituality and Authority

Spiritual life and the exercise of authority are both rooted in power dynamics. Power is the intended and desired effects one causes in the world.[17] In machismo, the distortions are unquestionably related to social and power relationships. These distortions correlate well with Shuster's argument of the distortion of the structure and will. From my analysis of the data, I suggest that the main issue of machismo in the male/male relationship has to do with distortions of the will. In machismo relationships among males,

---

13. Lingenfelter and Mayers, *Ministering Cross-Culturally*.
14. Prather, "Hispanic American," 34.
15. Shuster, *Power, Pathology, Paradox*.
16. Shuster, *Power, Pathology, Paradox*, 215.
17. Shuster, *Power, Pathology, Paradox*, 156.

there is an innate desire to demonstrate superiority over others males. For example, a male pastor with more accrued power (resources, money, education, experience) looks down on another male, proving he is more successful. Shuster asserts that every human being strives to find significance through power.

The distortion of structures describes how "a good thing" can be warped by one's will to control and dominate others. Ministry is a good example of how this distortion happens with machismo. Andean Pentecostal pastors have used ministry to control others; machismo becomes the vehicle whereby the will is imposed upon others.

In summary, Shuster provides insights into the degree of dysfunction that occurs when males and/or females look for significance and meaning through power. A corrective to this tendency can be found in a reframing of our notions of power. Instead of taking power to oneself, one should look at giving power to others, the powerless, the weak and outcast.[18]

Malleability as Renewal

Another theme worth considering is that of conformity. To resist conformity to the mold of the present order is an emphatic command in the Pauline letter to the Romans (Rom 12:1–3).

Impact on Character

Since transformation is an inner process that impacts the way leaders relate to God and others, it seems reasonable to suggest that renewal brings forth a reorientation in spirituality and interpersonal relationships. These significant changes are congruent with the theme of sanctification—which Paul's plea seems to suggest.

Since the call to renewal is a recurring reminder to those who believe that they should live in contrast to the norms of this world (culture), I suggest that malleability is an important factor in this process. Moreover, a call for transformation (metamorphosis) provides a robust correlation to what malleability offers because of suffering. Shuster rightly asserts this in the following:

---

18. Lingenfelter, *Leading Cross-Culturally*, 117.

> Now Scriptures presents the mind as either renewed by God or darkened by Satan (2 Cor 4:4); and our deception is certain if the mind is not renewed (Jer 17:9; Isa 44:20; Titus 3:3; Heb 3:13) . . . that is not to say that renewal does not change behavior—indeed it does and must—but part of its very transcendence is that behavior as judged by one's own or other's standard cannot serve as an ultimate.[19]

Based on the above, it seems that relying on malleability could become a challenge for transformation because the human tendency is to seek to control as an end in itself. This pervasive fluidity of machismo might be counteracted by the ongoing "renewing of our minds" in order to be truly redeemed.

Impact on Authenticity

Becoming agents of transformation requires that men and women have a relentless desire for ongoing spiritual refinement.[20] This desire produces a deep sense of authenticity that openly acknowledges both victories and failures—a more stable and matures way of relating to others. Authenticity is a critical trait in unmasked leaders who challenge and respond to the flawed images of culture.

This sense of renewal does not suggest an eradication of machismo; on the contrary, it should promote its submission to God's will—"the essential goal, condition and content of the Christian life."[21] This signifies what transforming culture should be like, when leaders in any given context do not conform to culture but respond as true agents of change. These leaders, whose authenticity allows to them to be strong when their power is perfected in weakness, become the antithesis to the culture of machismo.

Thus, malleability should not be used to hide weakness, but weakness and vulnerability should be openly shared resulting in an authentic orientation to God and others—a true transformation.[22]

19. Shuster, *Power, Pathology, Paradox*, 205–6.
20. Shuster, *Power, Pathology, Paradox*.
21. Shuster, *Power, Pathology, Paradox*, 110.
22. Trebesch, *Isolation*, 51. My findings suggest that even though Andean leaders are unmasked through crises; they learn to appropriately play the machismo game without being entangled in the flawed images it imposes on them. They are able to relate with other leaders under machismo code. In this process, I suggest that they become agents of transformation in their respective contexts.

Malleability Factors: Towards Inclusiveness

Latina theologian, Elsa Tamez, asserts that "machismo is an ideology in which women and men are victims and therefore, we all should fight against it."[23] I concur with this rationale as long as our "fight" relates to the way we include "the other."[24] Volf suggests that men and women of faith should hear the voice of the Spirit of embrace calling us "into being community that embody and through their practices transmit the will to embrace." Put differently, men and women who truly confess faith in Christ must engage in a fight against machismo through embracing and including instead of rejecting or excluding others.

Malleability breaks down the walls of exclusion and rejection that our cultures impose on men and women alike. Following Volf's argument, our confrontation with exclusion should be undergirded by a will to embrace "the other." Only then will the "fight" against machismo find its true purpose, leading us to become communities of inclusion and embrace in true obedience to Christ and his word.[25]

Three central factors that trigger malleability are pivotal in the transformation of machismo with the female factor as the hinge, bringing spirituality and functional relationship into the picture. Theologian Catalina de Padilla asserts that the significance of "recognizing that cultural assumptions in regards to women have been non-inclusive in the theologizing and hermeneutics."[26]

Thus, this study of machismo suggests that an adequate missiological reflection on this issue is necessary. This endeavor should provide new alternatives and perspectives for a more integrated and inclusive partnership in congregational and family social interactions. The following topics aim to present reflection on spirituality relative to issues of authority and power.

Summary

This chapter has introduced and expanded upon themes of missiological import that have emerged from my research and case studies.

---

23. Padilla and Tamez, *La Relacion*.
24. Volf, "Living with the Other," 8–25.
25. Volf, *Exclusion and Embrace*.
26. Volf, *Exclusion and Embrace*, 21.

Devoted to Christ

A transformation framework describing the interplay between unmasking, identification, malleability and reorientation carries missiological implications as they relate to the larger issues of suffering (unmasking) and renewal (malleability), two motifs that seem to undergird the entire process, and which are critical to the Christian story.

I have shown that these motifs carry broad and practical implications in the lives of Andean pastors, and leadership practice in general. The data reveals that interpersonal relationships, the very grist of leadership, are affected through variations in the leaders' behaviors, attitudes and interactions, all of which are informed perceptions of power and control.

Suffering and renewal, while not quantifiable, bear fruit in the lives of people in their grip, often dismantling skewed notions of power.

This study has shown the transformative potential of these missiological motifs in the lives of pastors. It is not too far a stretch to consider that the dynamics of suffering and renewal, though variably expressed, would have similar transformative power in other cultural contexts.

11

There is No Such Thing as "Honor" or "Honor Cultures"

A Missiological Reflection on Social Honor

CHRISTOPHER L. FLANDERS

Introduction

Honor is trendy these days. At least, that seems the case when surveying the quickly growing missiological literature that addresses honor (and shame) issues.[1] Though even the most ardent advocate would not see such as a "silver bullet" for missional practice or missiological theory, increased attention to honor-shame dynamics represents a critical change in missiology. This is so since the topic of honor has been frequently understudied, and perhaps just as often, completely ignored. Thus, such increased attention is an important and a welcome trend, which will certainly move

---

1. See, for example, Flanders, *About Face*; Pattison, *Shame*; Wu, *Saving God's Face*; Georges, *3D Gospel*; Michke, *Global Gospel*. Dissertations that address this area include Flanders, "About Face"; Persons, "Face Dynamics"; Levasheff, "Jesus of Nazareth." Also, note Tennent, *Theology*; Rynkiewich, *Soul, Self, and Society*, who both devote substantive sections that engage honor/shame issues. The recently published *Global Dictionary of Theology* has entries for both "Face" and "Shame." Finally, though not specifically Christian, there exists the explosion of interest and publications in the area of face and facework theory, e.g., Dominici and Littlejohn, *Facework*; Ting-Toomey, *Challenge of Facework*.

missiology past the "blind spot" that has often existed in this area.[2] Indeed, such issues represent what I consider one of the greatest missiological challenges of the early twenty-first century.[3]

That the topic of honor (and shame) has become du jour in missiological circles today does not signal that it has established itself as a core component of the missiological syllabus. Whether this new interest becomes more than merely a passing trend will depend upon rigorous missiological engagement. I attempt here to offer such an engagement. In particular, I argue that the missiological community must pay close attention to what the "experts" (anthropologists) have said about the area. This is so since, historically, missiological use of the honor-shame framework has been derivative, borrowed directly from the anthropological literature on honor.

Relying significantly upon another discipline, however, comes with certain risks. One challenge is reliance on outdated theory—that is, missiology based upon previously accepted but now superseded anthropological theory. Michael Rynkiewich aptly notes about this general tendency that often, while missiology "was looking the other way, anthropology walked off in a different direction, and the world itself took some strange turns."[4] The unfortunate result, Rynkiewich suggests, is that missiology taught in seminaries and mission training institutions is often profoundly outdated.[5]

What is true on a general level in missiology is particularly true of mission literature that deals with honor. Elsewhere, I have written about how this occurred regarding missiological literature that addressed the topics of shame and guilt.[6] Much missiological writing on shame and guilt assumed early anthropological theory as foundational. Yet, missiologists, failed to update their own discussions as the anthropological literature on shame and guilt gradually rejected much (if not most!) of the earlier anthropological theory. Here I attempt the same type of survey, focusing

---

2. Mischke, *Global Gospel*.

3. I say this for two important reasons. First, a Western lack of awareness of honor/shame issues has impacted negatively how we have read the bible (see, for example, Richards and O'Brien, *Misreading Scripture with Western Eyes*; DeSilva, *Hope of Glory*). Second, engaging honor/shame issues more directly will authorize non-Western Christians to own a local theological voice more confidently.

4. Rynkiewich, *Soul, Self, and Society*, xi.

5. Rynkiewich, *Soul, Self, and Society*, xii.

6. See chapter 3 of my book, *About Face*, in which I discuss at length how recent anthropology has moved beyond, and in some areas rejected the earlier theories of guilt and shame advocated by Ruth Benedict and Margaret Mead.

Flanders—There is No Such Thing as "Honor" or "Honor Cultures"

instead upon the topic of honor. In effect, missiology seized upon a dated notion of honor (i.e., honor as external, competitive, masculine, zero-sum) associated with putative "honor cultures." This created a convention of dividing cultures into "honor cultures" (or shame cultures, or face cultures) that contrasted with non-honor cultures (which, generally, were assumed to be modern Western cultures).

I intend to provide the contemporary missiological conversation regarding honor with a refresh of sorts, to bring current missiological theory into conversation with the updated anthropological theories regarding honor.

Challenges of Honor

To the ears of modern Western people, the term honor may sound outdated, perhaps even primitive. It hearkens us back to a foreign world, one of warriors, royalty, and aristocracy. No longer do we engage in duels because another has impugned our honor. To hear someone degrade our mother may lead us to chuckle rather than feel insult ("What do you mean? My mother doesn't even own a pair of army boots!"). In fact, we may have difficulty understanding how people can react with such intensity to statements that, though designed to insult us, we know not to be true. Yet, this seemingly antiquated notion we term honor may be more present in our lives than we might suppose.

Though many in our modern American society might dismiss personal honor outright, many of the same people would bristle if called a "wimp" or a "slut."[7] Even though President Bush obscured the notion by wrapping it in the language of good and evil, his call to the nation in response to the terrorist acts of September 11 clearly emanated from not only a sense of retributive justice but also from the need to defend the corporate honor of the nation.[8] If the ccontemporary discussions are to be believed, people in cultures "everywhere conduct their lives in milieu that are saturated with ideas about prestige—or standing, status, social honor, distinction."[9] Indeed, the very concept of self-esteem is honor-laden (a personal subjective honor judgment). Honor, it seems, is something that concerns us all.

---

7. Bowman, "Lost Sense of Honor," 6.
8. Bowman, "Lost Sense of Honor," 10.
9. Hatch, *Respectable Lives*.

Yet, just as honor is ubiquitous, so too is it baffling. The more one looks at this phenomenon in the literature, the more one is struck by the complexity and, at times, seemingly contradictory behavior that is subsumed under the rubric of honor.[10] Anthropologist Michael Herzfeld observes that the English term honor is in fact an inefficient gloss that covers a great variety of indigenous terminological systems.[11] His point is that there is no such thing as "honor"-only honors of various types and cultural specificity. Consequently, to delve into the study of social honor is to find oneself in a very expansive and, oftentimes, very confusing place.

An observation from anthropologist Elvin Hatch highlights one aspect of the inherent difficulties involved in discussing honor. Hatch notes a naïve and damaging assumption present in anthropological literature of honor, the *a priori* assumption that honor is a "relatively self-evident" concept.[12] Because they think they already know what constitutes honor or honor cultures, *what* they actually think and their basic assumptions remain unexamined. The result is that their specific notions of honor remains unanalyzed and open to tacit theoretical assumptions that do not proceed from critical studies or intentional analysis. Such precludes us from seeing the inner logic and specificity of honor systems and misattributing certain dynamics to honor when such is not the actual case. Therefore, we often think we already know what honor is, when in fact we do so based on a priori assumptions, not thoughtful examination. Thus, it is a critical first step to invest effort in understanding honor properly.

Dynamics of Honor and Honor Systems

A Definition of Honor

At its core, honor is about approval.[13] An individual gains approval from either self or society. Approval, in turn, is actually a category of formal evaluation. Therefore, regardless of the source or object, honor is at its core

---

10. Keating, "Honor and Statification," 399.

11. Herzfeld, "Honor and Shame," 339. Though Herzfeld was referring primarily to the study of honor within the discipline of anthropology, the same definitional confusion seems to occur in several disciplines.

12. Hatch, "Theories of Social Honor," 341–53.

13. Milner, *Status and Sacredness*, 30.

a positive evaluative attribution.[14] Though it may be expressed in a variety of forms, honor always rests upon ideals of some type of excellence. The measure of this excellence will vary over time and culture (e.g., moral virtue, success in battle, amount of financial resources, sexual prowess, or consistency with a personal code of conduct). Though variable, honor "provides a nexus between the ideals of a society and their reproduction in the individual through his aspiration to personify them."[15] This moral dimension of honor provides the foundation for any honor code.[16] Additionally, honor is never a single notion but rather a "conceptual field within which people find the means to express their self-esteem or their esteem for others."[17]

Honor, then, is inherently dynamic (it is considerably variable), positive (it is always about esteem), and ethical (it is an expression of certain notions of virtue, the good, and the excellent). What we term "honor" provides a critical link between the different positive social values of a culture, connecting them together into a coherent meta-category of evaluation. The enduring power of the concept of honor lies in this inclusive nature, bringing multiple positive moral notions together into a single evaluative category. Honor, to use Gilmore's term, is a "bundle of virtues."[18] Thus, a practical and cogent definition of honor is: a positive evaluation based upon recognition of virtue.

The Function of Honor

A rigorous engagement with the topic of honor must ask the basic question of the function of honor, i.e., what does honor do. What is its social and cultural "cash value"? One way to get at this question of function is to ask what would a society without notions of honor look like. Such a society, by necessity, would need to refrain from any moral or evaluative judgments. For, the moment a person makes a judgment of value or preference (e.g.,

---

14. Herzfeld, "Honor and Shame," 341.

15. Pitt-Rivers, *Fate of Shechem*, 1. Taylor comments appropriately on the essential connection between honor and excellence, "suggesting that we see all these diverse aspirations (for honor) as forms of a craving which is ineradicable from human life. We have to be rightly placed in relation to the good" (Taylor, *Sources of the Self*, 44).

16. Taylor, *Pride, Shame, and Guilt*; Stewart, *Honor*.

17. Persistiany and Pitt-Rivers, "Introduction," 1–17.

18. Gilmore, "Introduction," 2–21.

this is good, that is excellent, these things are desirable), a category in opposition to this original category is automatically created (e.g., this is bad, that is inferior, those are undesirable). When a person or social body associates with or possesses that virtue or "good," it and others will begin to engage in a positive evaluation, thus producing honor. Ancient Greek culture, as Dodds notes, operated with this binary moral evaluation of human action.[19] Moreover, no type of human social organization exists that does not make at least some evaluatory judgments of this sort. Since excellence is constitutive part of honor, any claim to excellence is, by definition, an honor-generating act. Honor is "an elementary property of human beings" that results from prescriptions of moral behavior.[20] In discussing the effect honor has on creating stratification, Pitt-Rivers notes "honor is the basis of preference."[21] It would be equally true, it seems, to conclude that preference is the basis for honor. In this evaluative sense, honor is the by-product of the unending human project of placing value upon things. Personal identity, social interaction, and the moral nature of community all require that we assign value to ourselves and to others.[22] Honor is thus an irreducible component of life in a world of preferences and judgments.

Honor also functions as an inherent aspect of human relationality. "All people share the universal need to gain the respect or esteem of others, since without it they can not as easily elicit the help of others . . . the foundations of social life rest in part on the universal need for respect, esteem, approval and honor."[23] I need your help—unless I have your esteem, I may very well not get the assistance I require. Esteeming others highly predisposes them to provide reciprocal help while being approved by others increases the likelihood of eliciting their help later. Honor in this way functions as a relational lubricant that makes social relations more effective and less threatening. My extending of relationship or assistance becomes a tacit, perhaps explicit, demonstration of my approval of you. Human relationality, in part, contributes to the creation of systems of honor.

The distinctions and classifications that are necessary products of social honor provide meaning and significance to our lives. As Bourdieu

---

19. That is, all conduct falls into either one of two categories, "kalon" (honorable) or "aischron" (shameful). See Dodds, *Greeks and the Irrational*, 26.

20. Kressel and Wikan, "More on Honor and Shame," 146.

21. Dodds, *Greeks and the Irrational*, 3.

22. Penman, "Facework in Communication," 20–23.

23. Goode, *Celebration of Heroes*, vii.

notes, "these principles of division are common to all the agents of the society and make possible the production of a common, meaningful world, a common-sense world."[24] The result of adjudicating between what is honorable and what is not "functions as a sort of social orientation, a 'sense of one's place,' guiding the occupants of a given place in social space."[25] Honor functions as a compass, orienting and guiding people through society.

Another important function of honor is that it animates the moral code of a society. This is not simply due to crass preoccupation with public opinion.[26] Ashley notes[27] that honor has a power which other singular moral virtues lack. It stands alone as something that resists all moral vice for to be a person of honor is to uphold the highest virtues and moral standards of a given society. In this way, honor provides the crucial motivational link between conceptual excellence and real-world behavior. What honor consists of (the elements of excellence or morality) is brought together with a sense (the affects associate with honor, e.g., pride, sense of honor, feelings of self respect, shame, guilt, etc.) of whether or not I am in fact living up to these particular noble standards.

Honor also function as a type of social power.[28] Honor bestows upon its owner certain advantages.[29] Goode's helpful work on prestige (honor) as a form of social control is essentially an extended commentary on how "granting or withdrawing prestige or esteem controls the actions of both individuals and groups."[30] Both Milner and Goode write of honor as social control and the ways by which status differentiation underwrites and perpetuates all forms of social strata. Status power of this form results from approval and disapproval and is expressed in the form of sanctions.[31] It involves both the dimension of human agency but also produces biased

---

24. Bourdieu, *Distinction*, 468.
25. Bourdieu, *Distinction*, 466.
26. Concern for what others think about us does often influence human behavior to a considerable degree. Among the ancient Greeks, for example, the "strongest moral force (was) not the fear of god, but respect for public opinion, *aidos*" (Dodds, *Greeks and the Irrational*, 18).
27. French, "Honor, Shame, and Identity," 2.
28. French, "Honor, Shame, and Identity," 23, 27.
29. French, "Honor, Shame, and Identity," 26.
30. French, "Honor, Shame, and Identity," 15.
31. French, "Honor, Shame, and Identity," 52.

structural systems.[32] It is the granting or withholding of honor that controls considerably how people and groups act.[33]

A related dimension of honor involves exchange. Honor constitutes an overall measure of a person's value to other people, especially their value as a partner in social exchange, and it is useful mainly for gaining the cooperation of other people. The symbolic capital of honor thus serves as *credit* in ongoing exchange relations. Equals want to exchange favors with an honorable person, superiors want to be a patron, and inferiors want to become clients. Indeed, honor is "the backbone of the system of patronage" where the constant seeking of honor, attachment to honor, and exchanging of honor constitute basic competitive impulses in honor systems.[34] Honor indexes both our reliability and our capacities to do things for others based on wealth, power, and connections. People will be loyal to honorable leaders because they protect and provide for followers, treat them justly, and display virtuous character traits likely to produce benefits for followers. Honorable followers in turn owe their leaders unshakable loyalty. Patrons and clients gauge one another's reliability by honor, and honoring their obligations in turn increases their honor.[35]

When viewed from the perspective of function, honor appears to be "social capital par excellence."[36] It is a commodity that can bring great benefits. It can get us preferential seating, lower prices, and many types of deferential treatment. It is also a force, the possession of which can empower the owner of honor to bring about desired results, whether by subtle influence or overt control or force. It also constitutes a fundamental role in the formation of our social world.

The history of honor in Anthropology

At least since the early twentieth century, anthropologists have offered definitions of honor and limited discussions about the topic.[37] Yet, honor,

---

32. French, "Honor, Shame, and Identity," 27.
33. French, "Honor, Shame, and Identity," 15.
34. French, "Honor, Shame, and Identity," 506–7.
35. Monsma, "Meaning of Honor," 10.
36. Monsma, "Meaning of Honor," 35.
37. Monsma, "Meaning of Honor," 13.

though acknowledged, remained peripheral as a topic of analysis in anthropological studies.[38]

The publication in 1965 of the landmark study by Jean G. Peristiany, *Honor and Shame: The Values of Mediterranean Society*, brought honor to the very center of anthropological investigation. This tour de force set the stage for all subsequent ethnographic investigations of honor, particularly so in the study of the regions of the Mediterranean and southern Europe.[39]

It is possible to trace the theme of honor as a topic of anthropological inquiry in two phases.[40] The earliest phase begins with Peristiany's volume on honor and subsequent literature that emerges is quite substantial. Scholars point to three specific works that form the core literature of this early period: the pioneering work of Peristiany, and the volumes by Pitt-Rivers and Campbell.[41]

One distinct mark of these early writings on honor is that of the cultural unity of the Mediterranean world. This model posited that a dominant concern for honor (and avoidance of shame) characterized this distinct cultural area. This cultural archetype presented by these scholars viewed the peoples of the large region of cultures bordering the Mediterranean as "united by a pervasive and relatively uniform value system based upon complementary codes of honor and shame."[42]

The type of honor presented was of a particular kind. Specifically, honor assumed by these studies involved a "sex-linked, binary opposition in which honor is (was) associated with men and shame with women."[43] Honor was intrinsically bound up in male ideology, sexuality, and competition. It was public, competitive, and male. This early understanding of honor would become the assumed definition of honor, functioning as a type of definitional "orthodoxy" and the basis for ensuing discussions regarding honor.

Following this early phase, a critique emerged, taking issue with several earlier assumptions. The earlier approach of Peristiany, Pitt-Rivers, and

---

38. Monsma, "Meaning of Honor," 3.

39. Coombe underscores this impact by noting that no topic "has been as definitive of the ethnography of Mediterranean societies than an enduring concern with the cultural values of honor and shame" (Coombe, "Barren Ground," 221–22).

40. Gilmore, "Introduction," 2–21, provides a helpful introduction and general survey of the anthropological literature.

41. Gilmore, "Introduction."

42. Gilmore, "Introduction," 2.

43. Brandes, "Reflections on Honor and Shame," 122.

Devoted to Christ

Gilmore led to a view of honor that was essentially static and totalizing. That is, that honor was identified with a single, dominant honor discourse, which remained unchallenged in a given culture. This led to a singular view of honor functioning in the production of cultural consensus and coherence. Such a view, however, all but excluded the possibility of seeing other definitions of honor at work in the same cultural context. Subsequent studies made it clear that in these cultures, several distinct honor discourses existed alongside the assumed dominant honor discourse.[44] Honor, it turned out, was not univocal. Sensitive studies that looked at other types of honor discovered many different honor discourses, definitions, and practices.

Another major point of contention with the earlier studies was the issue of how honor and maleness were related. Clearly, the earliest "orthodox" model directly connected honor and an ideology of maleness. Lindisfarne notes the "disarmingly consistent . . . focus on competition between dominant men and the passive subordination of women" as an example of this accepted orthodoxy.[45] Critical of this type of male-related honor, Wikkan leveled a scathing critique against this "orthodoxy" by highlighting notions of honor and shame from a female perspective. Granted that the male-based definition had gained great acceptance, she asks whether it can really be the case that females do not have any independent honor. Wikkan contends that a definition of honor based upon selective discourse (i.e., only the dominating male discourse) would by definition exclude women, since honor was about bravado, competition, and exercise of male power. The very possibility of a female honor is excluded by circularity in reasoning.[46]

---

44. Baroja pointed out, in an interesting study of sixteenth and seventeenth century Spanish culture, that while in some respects there was a level of coherence, there was also significant tension, even outright contradiction between competing versions of honor held by differing segments of Spanish society (Baroja, "Religion," 91). Abu-Lughod's ethnography of Bedouin culture similarly identifies conflicting currents of honor in the recognized dominant honor code and forms that subverted that code with alternate sentiments. Honor even among as homogenous a culture as Bedouin society was diverse and multivalent.

45. Lindisfarne, "Gender, Shame, and Culture," 248.

46. Others have concurred with Wikkan's critique (see Coombe, "Barren Ground"; Gilmore, "Honor and Shame"; Lindisfarne, "Gender, Shame, and Culture"). Miller described the medieval Icelandic notion of honor that, although somewhat gendered, was "not obsessively focused on the condition of the female genitalia and did not lead to an ideal or a reality of female sequestration" (Miller, *Humiliation*, 118). He also notes that for the Icelandic males, honor was generally not dependent upon women (Miller, *Humiliation*, 119). Gilmore's study among the Andalusian identified a male honor that does not primarily depend upon sexual functioning, but consists more in economics,

Wikkan argues successfully that females also participate in honor, thus overturning how male-dominated definitions of honor in earlier studies.

The literature of this period challenged other notions. Honor, for example, was not always a zero-sum and competitive game. Sometimes it was transactional and cooperative, based upon beneficial exchange.[47] Likewise, honor was not always related to hierarchical contexts but also existed as a prominent dynamic among equals.[48] This second generation of honor studies broke through the provincialism and over-generalizations that resulted from the first phase of anthropological studies on Mediterranean cultures. These later studies have shown that many other values constitute the honor codes within the various Mediterranean cultures, thus demonstrating that honor was "more complicated and variable—in effect, richer—than the pioneers suspected."[49]

The important point for this study is simply this-earliest missiological discussions regarding honor relied upon anthropological theory of this earlier period. Subsequent anthropological study on honor challenges and rejected many fundamental assumptions of this earliest period. The phenomenon that Rynkiewich noted had indeed occurred—anthropology moved on, developing more nuanced and sophisticated understandings of honor, while missiology remained firmly attached to the outdated honor definitions and theories.

The Components And Dynamics Of Honor

Here I offer a brief survey of some of these nuanced conversations regarding honor and how the more recent literature can inform the missiological conversation. There are several enduring enigmas in the literature on honor. One consists of just how to connect two similar yet very different manifestations of honor. That is, how do what are often termed "external" and "internal" honor relate to one another? There is frequent discussion centering on whether honor is more like personal virtue (honor as a moral notion) or whether honor is more about social standing or public opinion

---

honesty, and proper interrelational exchange.

47. Miller, *Humiliation*, 100.
48. Gilmore, "Honor and Shame," 91.
49. Gilmore, "Honor and Shame," 91.

(honor as status or reputation).⁵⁰ It is often not clear why a particular notion counts as honor while another does not.⁵¹

Internal and External Honor

Pitt-Rivers offers what, largely, has formed the basis for "orthodoxy" in the anthropological literature on honor. Honor consists of "a sentiment, a manifestation of that sentiment in conduct, and the evaluation of this conduct by others."⁵² Honor is "at the same time a matter of moral conscience and a sentiment on the one hand, and on the other, a fact of repute and precedence."⁵³ Here, Pitt-Rivers highlights two critical dimensions—one that exists outside the person and one that is internal. This bipartite approach highlights what many have termed the *outer* or *external* and the *inner* or *internal* dimensions of honor. It is this that distinguishes two separate dimensions of the single entity (viz., honor), which is the most common approach to understanding honor. As Stewart remarks, any "analysis that does not connect the two aspects of honor closely to each other starts life with a marked handicap."⁵⁴ Honor is both a public, external reality but also a subjective, internal experience. Both dynamics need to inform responsible discussions regarding honor dynamics.

The notion of external honor points to something that exists outside of oneself. It is wrapped up in what others think and in the type of person they believe another to be. If someone accuses me of stealing and I become self-conscious about how this evaluation will affect what others think about me, it is the external type of honor with which I am concerned. In this type of situation, honor refers to the positive evaluation of a person's character or actions by others outside the person's own self. This can be seen by how one may replace the term honor with notions such as "reputation," "repute," or "a good name." These fit in place of honor quite well and attest to the public nature, the external character, of this side of honor. I may or may not be guilty of stealing but honor of this type is not my possession and, to

---

50. Keating, "Honor and Statification," 401.

51. Keating, "Honor and Statification," 5.

52. Pitt-Rivers, *Fate of Shechem*, 503. Stewart quotes Patterson, a well-know sociologist, who designates Pitt-Rivers's definition the "communis opinio" in the social sciences. See Stewart, *Honor*, 13.

53. Stewart, *Honor*, 5.

54. Stewart, *Honor*, 12.

that extent, is something which I cannot control. It is specifically dependent upon factors outside myself and may or may not relate to what is actually the case. The only reality upon which this external type of honor depends is the reality of public opinion. Some social entity that exists outside my own self forms the court of reputation that will render a verdict of either honor or dishonor.

As Stewart notes, the second type of honor is of a very different kind.[55] The honor of this second type is quite closely associated with ones' own self or character, one's own dignity. Two things make this quite different from the first type of honor. First, my response of anger and personal injury is not necessarily tied to what any outsider thinks. Indeed, the insult may very well happen in private yet the sting may be just as intense as that of the loss of public reputation. My personal reputation as to whether I am in fact a coward is not the substantive issue. Whether or not the charge was true depends on variables quite independent from the insulting remark. Additionally, what I know is in fact really the case is not the central issue. That is, I may know myself *not* to be a coward. I may be fully convinced in my own mind that this charge is spurious and completely off the mark. Yet, I still feel that my honor has been damaged in some way. How is this the case? This second notion, that of internal honor, is one quite closely related to self in a way fundamentally different from that of external honor.

Stewart draws upon the work of Moritz Liepmann, an expert in German criminal law writing during the early part of the twentieth century[56] who astutely observes that if one defines honor as a "possession of certain qualities, specifically those qualities that determine a person's worth" then it is difficult to understand how in the scenario above, honor has actually been damaged. Another person may challenge these virtues as much as they like yet if those qualities that determine one's honor remain unchanged, then nothing in fact has been damaged. Theoretically, one is just as honorable after the insult as before. No honor has been impugned and therefore there is no criminal offense.

Leipmann therefore develops the idea of subjective and objective honor. Using these twin concepts, he explains a way that such honor may be truly injured. When insulted in front of others, one's objective honor (reputation) has been damaged. Likewise, a person's subjective honor,

---

55. Stewart, *Honor*, 11.
56. Stewart, *Honor*, 14.

their "sense of their own worth" is harmed when another issues an insult.[57] What the world thinks of me (objective honor) and the estimation I have for myself (subjective honor) are of considerable value to me and are both potentially injured upon insult, whether private or public. Both, however, are in fact types of honor.

Honor as a Claim-Right

How a personal insult is damaging to one's "subjective" or "internal" honor brings us to a very particular aspect of honor not often noted in the anthropological literature, but clearer in the philosophical discussions of honor. This is that honor is fundamentally an issue of a *claim-right*.[58] Simply viewing honor as internal and external (whether Liepmann's view or any other version of a bipartite theory of honor) cannot account for the prevalent feature of honor systems which we term "insult." To call me a coward cannot (at least, logically, it seems) affect my internal honor, though it of course may very well affect my external honor. Yet, it is by such an insult that people often experience a great offense against personal honor. Stewart suggests that to understand the dynamics of honor (and insult) properly we must view the notion as a type of claim-right. That is, at its core, honor is a social right. More specifically, honor is the possession or claim to possess a right to certain types of behavior toward myself. It is "a right that something be done by another."[59] The bearer of this right, for whatever specific reasons, has something about him, which gives him the right to respect.[60] What actually constitutes the basis of this right can of course vary widely (e.g., social standing, virtue, physical properties of different kinds, etc.). The world, on the other hand, has the obligation to offer a certain type of respectful behavior toward the bearer of the right.

This explains why both personal insult (assault on internal honor) and a lack of respect from society (failure to support external honor) are problematic. I believe that, because I am a certain type of person or because I have done such and such, I am worthy of respect. Society in fact owes such to me. Pitt-Rivers's earlier definition hinted at this when he noted that honor involves the "estimation of his own worth, his *claim* to pride,

57. Stewart, *Honor*, 15.
58. Stewart, *Honor*, 21.
59. Stewart, *Honor*, 21.
60. Stewart, *Honor*, 21.

but it also the acknowledgment of that claim, his excellence recognized by society, his *right* to pride."[61] Again, honor "implies not merely an habitual preference for a given mode of conduct, but the entitlement to a certain treatment in return."[62] Not to receive such honor produces frustration. The various experiences associated with the concept of honor then depend to a large degree upon this dynamic of being a claim-right.

Honor Code

An honor code consists in a series of judgments, expressed in terms of a set of standards about that which is good and approved and the sorts of behavior that should accompany this standard.

> The code of honor is a set of standards that has been picked out as having particular importance, that measures an individual's worth along some profoundly significant dimensions; and a member of the honor group who fails to met [sic] these standards is viewed not just as inferior but often also as despicable.[63]

The constitutive elements of any honor code include at least the following: 1) a definition of what constitutes honorable life/action; 2) the types of behaviors that constitute a breach in the honor code; 3) the remedial actions (if any) that are appropriate in order to deal with one's own impugned honor or that of another.

What function does the honor code play in honor systems? Friedrich[64] suggests that any honor code has two primary functional dimensions: the cognitive and pragmatic. An honor code functions as a conceptual framework "in terms of which phenomena are conceptualized and interpreted." Likewise, honor codes act to structure human action (encouraging specific honorable behavior) and prescribing how to terminate or resolve conflict or non-honorable action.[65]

The sources of the code may vary from culture to culture. In many places, it may be determined through community consensus and transmitted as a normal part of social responsibility. Alternately, in highly individualized

---

61. Stewart, *Honor*, 1.
62. Stewart, *Honor*, 1.
63. Stewart, *Honor*, 55.
64. Stewart, *Honor*, 284.
65. Stewart, *Honor*, 284.

cultures, it may become so privatized that it exists as an exclusive product and possession of the solitary individual. It may be idiosyncratic and not tied directly to any social unit outside the individual self. For example, Otto von Bismarck. He states,

> Gentlemen, my honor lies in no-one's hands but my own, and it is not something that others can lavish on me; my own honor, which I carry in my heart, suffices me entirely, and no-one is judge of it and able to decide whether I have it. My honor before God and men is my property, I give myself as much as I believe that I have deserved, and I renounce any extra.[66]

Stewart discusses the rise of a "sense of honor" as playing a significant role in "the decline of honor" in Western culture; he notes how more stress is laid upon the sense of honor of the individual rather than the specific honor code available.[67] Rather, it seems, what has actually happened is simply that a highly individualized Western version of the person or self has taken over the primary role of definition of the honor code. The privately defined personal honor code becomes primary instead of an honor code derived from a larger social unit. A societal honor code becomes a more personal "sense of honor" which is then radicalized and subsequently becomes the individual's private honor code. Honor did not decline. Rather, it was reconfigured, changing cultural shape.

The components which may constitute a given honor code are conceivably as variable and potentially diverse as are the cultures of the world: the Bedouin honor code,[68] for whom honor depends upon the supreme values of autonomy and freedom; the Pohnpein honor code that posits self-depletion as central to gaining honor as subordinating language is turned into superordination[69]; the complex code of the Illiadic culture of Homer that values public reputation and physical valor[70]; certain European cultures that place individual property rights as basic to the honor code[71]; Feudal French culture that defined honor in terms of personal courage and military ability while latter French bourgeois culture honor depended upon marital fidelity, sexual power, and discipline and reliability in public life

---

66. Otto von Bismarck quoted in Stewart, *Honor*, 52.
67. Stewart, *Honor*, 146.
68. Abu-Lughod, "Veiled Sentiments," 79.
69. Keating, "Honor and Stratification," 409.
70. Friedrich, "Sanity," 290.
71. Friedrich, "Sanity," 282.

and business; or present-day Andalusian where honor is essentially "social ethics," being honest and in particular, being sensitive to one's social obligations of reciprocity.[72] Other cultures place the practice of hospitality at the center of the honor code.[73] The point is simple—honor codes vary considerably in the particular ideals and notions that provide the contents of the general category of honor in any specific cultural configuration.

Honor Group

Closely associated with the notion of honor codes is that of the honor group. An honor group is simply that specific set of people following the same honor code who recognize each other as doing so.[74] Honor groups not only follow the same honor code but also often function as the keepers of the honor code, thus providing a social mechanism for their continuing viability. The honor group may also function as the "tribunal before which the claims of honor are brought, 'the court of reputation' as it has been called, and against its judgments there is no regress."[75]

Such a group may be relatively diffuse and broad. This could consist of an extended family, a particular stratum of society, or even an entire nation. Alternately, an honor group can be quite narrow and exclusive. Such is the case in the writings of Robert Ashley and Francis Bacon who limit the honor group to a very narrow clique, those whom are deemed noble-minded and sufficiently cultured.[76] The term honor group may be a misnomer, however, as sometimes the honor group may become so narrow that the individual itself essentially replaces the group, prescribing its own personal honor code and becoming the sole legitimate judge of personal honor. This is the modern autonomous version of highly individualized personal integrity honor. At the other extreme, in a highly collectivist context, the loss of honor may result in exclusion from the honor group.[77] Sometimes, in the hierarchy of a nuclear family or a nation, the honor of individual members is vitally connected to a single figure (father, king, etc.) whose personal honor stands for the honor the entire group. Such a principle of honor residing

72. Nye, *Masculinity*, 31–46.
73. Herzfeld, "As in Your Own House," 75.
74. Herzfeld, "As in Your Own House," 54.
75. Herzfeld, "As in Your Own House," 7.
76. Herzfeld, "As in Your Own House," 4.
77. Herzfeld, "As in Your Own House," 111.

in the head of the group was fundamental to European feudal systems and aristocracy.[78] This can explain how it is that even though members of a nation may not have particular fondness for their leader, yet a criticism of that head of state may be taken as an impugnment of national honor, and derivatively, personal honor as well. Honor groups can be powerful sources and legitimators of diffused honor.

There is No Such Thing as Honor-Only Honors

What can we take away from this brief review? First, it is clear from even a cursory survey, that honor in anthropology (and other disciplines) does not exist as a univocal topic. Rather, there is great diversity of how scholars frame the study of honor. Clearly, culture and social environment play a significant role in how honor manifests in particular contexts. To return to Herzfeld's basic contention, honor does not represent a single "thing" but rather a field of dynamics that varies widely. Second, though critical anthropological studies of honor began with a focus on the Mediterranean and have remained largely a topic of inquiry for non-western cultures, it is incorrect, therefore, to label such as "honor" cultures. That is, to seize upon the earliest (or any, for that matter!) single definition of honor that narrowly constrains honor dynamics (ignoring the great diversity of experiences that all properly fall under the rubric of honor) and then utilizes that definition to delineate "honor cultures" from other cultures is illegitimate. If one thing is clear, it is that the dynamic of honor (and shame) is present in all cultures and that the tag "honor culture" or "shame culture" is not only unhelpful but also inaccurate. To say it another way, there is no such thing as an honor culture. It is clear that honor dynamics exist universally. There is no analytically precise way to draw a line to indicate when a culture is or is not a so-called honor culture. What is more accurate is to understand that honor functions in culturally distinct ways in all cultural contexts. Missiology would be best served by eliminated the terminology of "honor culture" (or, for that matter, "shame culture") and focus instead on the specific honor-shame dynamics that are present in every cultural context.

---

78. Herzfeld, "As in Your Own House," 14.

Conclusion

Honor is a universal phenomenon. No culture or sub-culture lacks a notion of what is excellent, and this in turn produces the binary concepts of honor and dishonor (shame). Every culture does this. Given this ubiquity of social honor, we humans are inescapably *homo honorificus*.

Though there appear to be universal dynamics that create and regulate honor at one level, the specific shape of honor will vary widely, depending upon cultural context. Broadly generalizing based upon a stereotypical framework of ostensible "honor cultures" is incredibly irresponsible. Since this is so, in reality there is no such thing as honor, but only culturally specific honors. Indeed, in the biblical vision of Revelation, each nation brings in its own glory and honor into the heavenly city (Revelation 21:26). Because of this great honor variety, the study of honor requires focused, culturally specific, and linguistically nuanced approaches to understanding each cultural manifestation of this important universal dynamic.[79]

Beyond the call to stop using the definition of what constitutes honor and "honor cultures" from the early anthropological literature on honor, I wish to make an even bolder claim. I believe we must come to terms with the fact that *there is no such thing as honor cultures* if by that we mean a distinct type of culture that operates on honor dynamics in opposition to cultures that do not "do" honor. Each culture contains, necessarily, dynamics that inevitably produce honor, albeit honor in varying forms. Honor is universal. All cultures in reality are honor cultures.

The tendency to label cultures with this designation of "honor culture" may produce at least two negative outcomes. First, it can lead missionaries to fall for naïve stereotypes about what putative honor cultures are (and are not!). These caricatures can actually obscure real honor dynamics by the imposition of a foreign "honor culture" framework.

Potentially just as damaging, however, is the likely tendency to fail to look for honor dynamics in cultures that have not been traditionally included in the category of "honor culture" (or "shame culture"). Do we miss critical honor (and shame) dynamics in modern western cultures simply because we assume these not to be "honor cultures"? Such is extremely likely if we accept the myth of the disappearance of honor in the modern

---

79. Herzfeld, "As in Your Own House," 14.

West.[80] We, as a community of mission scholars and practitioners, would be wise to dispose of the label of "honor culture" completely.

Understanding that honor is a universal dimension of all cultures and that labeling cultures as "honor cultures" is both inaccurate and unhelpful, should alert missiologists and missionaries alike to pay closer attention to honor as a broad missiological issues. In particular, I suggest missionaries gain tools and develop a framework to do honor exegesis in their cultural context. Indeed, since honor is so materially critical for the functioning of cultures, I suggest missionaries pay special attention to several areas through honor lenses.

To understand a local culture's morality system requires attention to honor. Honor in whatever form it appears is always fused to personal and societal notions of what is good, noble, and excellent. As above, Gilmore's notion of honor as a "bundle of virtues." If a missionary wishes to understand the moral and ethical structure of a society, a focused study of that society's honor system would prove incredibly helpful. It would be a powerful first step to understanding important issues about the values and functioning of any culture.

Because of the important work of anthropologists and other scholars, we must critically re-read Scripture with honor lenses. These have brought to light the importance social honor has in the biblical texts. Often, lack of honor-awareness will lead missionaries and those they train to miss these important biblical dynamics.

Discipleship is also an honor-laden task. Crucial to effective discipleship is the reconstituting of the court of reputation. Whether self (internal honor) or other (external honor), ultimate honor must be that which comes from our God. As Paul wrote, "We rejoice in the hope of the honor that comes from God" (Rom 5:2). DeSilva reminds us of this important feature of much New Testament literature and the materially significant role that honor plays in this important work.[81] This type of work is only possible by those who both understand broadly honor systems and also take the time to learn the culturally specific dynamics of local honor systems.

Other important missiological questions involve honor considerations. How would a biblical theology of honor support or subvert a

---

80. That "honor and shame had largely become extinct in Western societies by 1900" is a preposterous claim by anthropologist Charles Stewart. It only makes sense if one defines honor extraordinarily narrowly along the lines of the earlier anthropological "orthodoxy." See Stewart, "Honor and Shame," 3.

81. See, for example, DeSilva, *Hope of Glory; Honor, Patronage, Kinship and Purity.*

particular cultural view of social honor. How can culturally produced honor codes and courts of reputation be infused with gospel values? Can the Christian community reframe the issues of honor and shame to reflect God's new kingdom? I believe those engaged in the mission of God can find in social honor a powerful cultural and biblical concept which, approached with sufficient critical awareness and determination, may lead us to new vistas of cultural understanding and fruitful kingdom ministry. But, we must always have in mind that there is no singular "honor" or such a thing as "honor culture." The diversity and dynamism of this basic social category requires missionaries and missiologists alike to broaden our definitions so we may more accurately and faithfully engage social honor.

Bibliography

Abu-Lughod, Lila. *Veiled Sentiments: Honor and Poetry in a Bedouin Society.* Berkeley, CA: University of California Press, 1986.
Adams, Richard Newbold. *Energy and Structure: A Theory of Social Power.* Austin, TX: University of Texas Press, 1975.
Akin Rabibhadana. "Bangkok Slum: Aspects of Social Organization." PhD diss., Cornell University, 1975.
———. *The Organization of Thai Society in the Early Bangkok Period 1782–1873.* Ithaca, NY: Cornell University Press, 1969.
Anderson, Stephen R. *Doctor Dolittle's Delusion: Animals and the Uniqueness of Human Language.* New Haven: Yale University Press, 2004.
Archer, Margaret. *Being Human: The Problem of Agency.* New York: Cambridge University Press, 2000.
Ashforth, Adam. *Witchcraft, Violence, and Democracy in South Africa,* Chicago: University of Chicago Press, 2005.
Audéoud, Martine, and Rubin Pohor. "Hope for the Christian Church through Global Incarnational Partnerships." *Lausanne Global Conversation Archives.* http://conversation.lausanne.org/resources/detail/11606.
Augsburger, David W. *Conflict Mediation Across Cultures.* Louisville: Westminster John Knox, 1992.
Barnard, H. Russell. *Research Methods in Anthropology.* Walnut Creek, CA: Altamira, 2002.
Barnett, Milton L. "Hiya, Shame, and Guilt: Preliminary Consideration of the Concepts as Analytical Tools for Philippine Social Science." *Philippine Sociological Review* 14 (1966) 271–82.
Baroja, Julio Caro. "Religion, World Views, Social Classes, and Honor During the Sixteenth and Seventeenth Centuries in Spain." In *Honor and Grace in Anthropology,* edited by J. Pitt-Rivers and J. G. Peristiany, 91–102. Cambridge Studies in Social and Cultural Anthropology 76. Cambridge, UK: Cambridge University Press, 1992.
Bartle, Neville. *Death, Witchcraft, and the Spirit World in the Highlands of Papua New Guinea: Developing a Contextual Theology in Melanesia.* Goroka, Papua New Guinea: Melanesia Institute, 2005.
———. "Developing a Contextual Theology in Melanesia with Reference to Death, Witchcraft, and the Spirit World." PhD diss., Asbury Theological Seminary, 2001.
Beck, Ulrich, and Elisabeth Beck-Gernsheim. *Individualization: Institutionalized Individualism and Its Social and Political Consequences.* London: Sage, 2002.

Bibliography

Benedict, Ruth. *The Chrysanthemum and the Sword*. Boston: Houghton Mifflin, 1946.
Berger, Peter, et al. *The Homeless Mind*. New York: Random House, 1973.
Bickerton, Derek. *Adam's Tongue: How Humans Made Language, How Language Made Humans*. New York: Hill and Wang, 2009.
Biehl, J. *Vita. Life in a Zone of Social Abandonment*. Berkeley, CA: University of California Press, 2005.
Boeck, F. de, and M. F. Plissart. *Kinshasa: Tales of the Invisible City*. Tervuren, Belgium: Royal Museum for Central Africa, 2004.
Bohannan, Laura. "Shakespeare in the Bush." *Natural History* 75.8 (1966) 28–33.
Bolman, Lee G., and Terrence E. Deal. *Reframing Organizations*. San Francisco: Jossey-Bass, 2008.
Bourdieu, Pierre. *Distinction: A Social Critique of the Judgement of Taste*. Translated by R. Nice. Cambridge: Harvard University Press, 1984.
Bowman, James. "The Lost Sense of Honor." *Public Interest* 149 (2002) 32–49.
Brandes, Stanley. "Reflections on Honor and Shame in the Mediterranean." In *Honor and Shame and the Unity of the Mediterranean*, edited by David D. Gilmore, 121–34. Washington, DC: American Anthropological Association, 1987.
Bright, John. *The Kingdom of God*. Nashville: Abingdon, 2010.
"Britain's Sun Calls Chirac a Worm." *Los Angeles Times* February 21, 2003, A6.
Brown, Andrew D., and W. T. Thomborrow. "Do Organizations Get the Followers They Deserve?" *Leadership and Organization Development Journal* 17 (1996) 5–11.
Brown, Michael. "Dark Side of the Shaman." *Natural History* 98.11 (1989) 8–11.
Brusco, Elizabeth E. *The Reformation of Machismo: Evangelical Conversion and Gender in Colombia*. Austin, TX: University of Texas Press, 1995.
Burns, James MacGregor. *Leadership*. New York: Harper and Row, 1978.
Bush, Luis, and Larry Lutz. *Partnering in Ministry: The Direction of World Evangelism*. Downers Grove, IL: InterVarsity, 1990.
Cairns, Douglas L. *Aidos: The Psychology and Ethics of Honor and Shame in Ancient Greek Literature*. Oxford: Clarendon, 1993.
Campbell, J. K. *Honor, Family, and Patronage: A Study of Institutions and Moral Values in a Greek Mountain Community*. Oxford: Oxford University Press, 1964.
Castañeda, Marina. *El Machismo Invisible*. Mexico: Grijalbo, 2002.
Chai Podhisita. "Buddhism and Thai World View." In *Traditional and Changing World View*, edited by Amara Pongsapich, et al., 25–53. Bangkok, Thailand: Chulalongkorn University Social Research Institute, 1985.
Chomsky, Noam. *Syntactic Structures*. The Hague: Mouton, 1957.
Collier, Paul. *The Bottom Billion: Why the Poorest Countries are Failing and What Can Be Done About It*. Oxford: Oxford University Press, 2007.
Coombe, Rosemary J. "Barren Ground: Re-Conceiving Honor and Shame in the Field of Mediterranean Ethnography." *Anthropologica* 32 (1990) 221–38.
Cooper, R. *Culture Shock Thailand*. Singapore: Times International, 1982.
Corwin, Gary. "Doing Diversity Well." *EMQ* 44 (2008) 416–17.
———. "Of Partnerships and Power Trips." *EMQ* 44 (2008). https://missionexus.org/of-partnerships-and-power-trips.
Covey Stephen R. *The 7 Habits of Highly Effective People*. Great Britain: Simon & Schuster UK, 1999.
Cox, Taylor H., Jr. *Creating the Multicultural Organization*. San Francisco: John Wiley, 2001.

Bibliography

———. "The Multicultural Organization." *Academy of Management Executive* 5 (1991) 34–47.
Creighton, Millie R. "Revisiting Shame and Guilt Cultures: A Forty-Year Pilgrimage." *Ethos* 18 (1990) 279–307.
Crouch, Andy. "The Return of Shame." *Christianity Today* 59 (2015) 32–40.
Davis, John R. *Poles Apart?* Bangkok: Kanok Bannasan, 1993.
De Cuéllar, Javier Pérez. "Our Creative Diversity: Report of the World Commission on Culture and Development." Paris: UNESCO, 1996.
Dean, Benjamin P. "Global Alliances as a Strategy for Proactive International Integration." *Lausanne World Pulse Archives*, November 2006. http://www.lausanneworldpulse.com/themedarticles.php/527.
Dennison, Jack. *City Reaching—A Road to Community Transformation*. Pasadena, CA: William Carey, 1999.
deSilva, David A. *Honor, Patronage, Kinship and Purity—Unlocking New Testament Culture*. Downers Grove, IL: InterVarsity, 2000.
———. *The Hope of Glory: Honor Discourse and New Testament Interpretation*. Collegeville, MN: Liturgical, 1999.
Dierck, Lorraine W. "Teams That Work: Leadership, Power, and Decision-Making in Multicultural Teams in Thailand." PhD diss., Biola University, 2007.
Dodds, E. R. *The Greeks and the Irrational*. Berkeley: University of California Press, 1959.
Domenici, Kathy, and Stephen W. Littlejohn. *Facework: Bridging Theory and Practice*. Thousand Oaks, CA: Sage, 2006.
Douglas, Mary. *In the Active Voice*. London: Routledge & Kegan Paul, 1982.
———. "Sorcery Accusations Unleashed: The Lele Revisited, 1987." *Africa* 69 (1999) 177–93.
Downes, Donna R. "Cultural Bias in a Mission Organization." In *Agents of Transformation*, 206–15. Grand Rapids, MI: Baker, 1996.
———. "The Globalization of Mission: Missiological Dream or Management Nightmare." PhD diss., Biola University, 2004.
Dye, Wayne T. "Toward a Cross-Cultural Definition of Sin." *Missiology* 4 (1976) 27–41.
Eberhard, David M., et al., eds. "Endangered Languages." In *Ethnologue: Languages of the World*. 22nd ed. Dallas, TX: SIL International, 2019. https://www.ethnologue.com/endangered-languages#LgEndgrEGIDS.
Edelman, Lester, et al. *Partnering: A Tool for USACE, Engineering, Construction, and Operations. Pamphlet 4: Alternative Dispute Resolution Series*. Fort Belvoir, VA: US Army Corps of Engineers Institute for Water Resources, 1991.
Edelmann, Robert J. *The Psychology of Embarrassment*. Chichester, UK: Wiley, 1987.
Eisenstadt, S. N., and L. Roniger. *Patrons, Clients, and Friends—Interpersonal Relations and the Structure of Trust in Society*. Cambridge, UK: Cambridge University Press, 1984.
Ellis, Bill. *Raising the Devil: Satanism, New Religions, and the Media*. Lexington, KY: University Press of Kentucky, 2000.
Elliston, Edgar J., and J. Timothy Kauffman. *Developing Leaders for Urban Ministries*. New York: Peter Lang, 1993.
Embree, J. F. "Thailand: A Loosely-Structured Social System." *American Anthropologist* 52 (1950) 181–93.
Evans-Pritchard, E. E. *Witchcraft, Oracles, and Magic Among the Azande*. Oxford: Oxford University Press, 1976.

Bibliography

Finley, Moses I. *The World of Odysseus*. London: Chatto and Windus, 1977.
Fishman, Joshua. *Reversing Language Shift*. Clevedon, UK: Multilingual Matters, 1991.
Flanders, Christopher L. "About Face: Reorienting Thai Face for Soteriology and Mission." PhD diss., Fuller Theological Seminary, 2005.
———. *About Face: Rethinking Face for Twenty-First-Century Mission*. Eugene, OR: Pickwick, 2011.
Fowler, Allan. *Striking a Balance: A Guide to Enhancing the Effectiveness of Non-Governmental Organizations in International Development*. London: Earthscan, 1999.
Fowler, James W. *Faithful Change: The Personal and Public Challenges of Postmodern Life*. Nashville, TN: Abingdon, 1996.
Foxcroft, Gary. "Supporting Victims of Witchcraft Abuse and Street Children in Nigeria." *Consortium for Street Children*. https://www.streetchildrenresources.org/wp-content/uploads/2013/03/supporting-victims-of-witchcraft-abuse-street-children-nigeria.pdf.
French, Peter A. "Honor, Shame, and Identity." *Public Affairs Quarterly* 16 (2002) 1–15.
Friedman, Thomas. *The World Is Flat: A Brief History of the Twenty-First Century*. New York: Farrar, Strauss, and Giroux, 2005.
Friedrich, Paul. "Sanity and the Myth of Honor: The Problem of Achilles." *Ethos* 5 (1977) 281–305.
Georges, Jayson. *The 3D Gospel: Ministry in Guilt, Shame, and Fear Cultures*. n.p.: Timē Press, 2014.
Geschiere, P. *The Modernity of Witchcraft: Politics and the Occult in Postcolonial Africa*. Charlottesville, VA: University Press of Virginia, 1997.
Gibbs, Eddie, and Ryan K. Bolger. *Emerging Churches: Creating Christian Community in Postmodern Cultures*. Grand Rapids, MI: Baker Academic, 2005.
Giddens, Anthony. *Central Problems in Social Theory*. Berkeley, CA: University of California Press, 1979.
———. *The Constitution of Society: Outline of the Theory of Structuration*. Oxford: Polity, 1984.
Gilmore, David, A. *Honor and Shame and the Unity of the Mediterranean*. Washington, DC: American Anthropological Association, 1987.
Girard, René. *I See Satan Fall Like Lightning*. Maryknoll, NY: Orbis, 2001.
———. *The Scapegoat*. Baltimore: John Hopkins University Press, 1986.
———. *Things Hidden Since the Foundation of the World*. Stanford, CA: Stanford University Press, 1987.
———. *Violence and the Sacred*. Baltimore: John Hopkins University Press, 1977.
Goffman, Erving. "On Face-Work: An Analysis of Ritual Elements in Social Interaction." *Psychiatry* 18 (1955) 213–31.
Goleman, Daniel. *Emotional Intelligence*. New York: Bantam, 1995.
Goode, William J. *The Celebration of Heroes: Prestige as Social Control*. Berkeley, CA: University of California Press, 1978.
Gravelle, Gilles. "Mission Reinvention: Why Some Leaders Think it Urgent." *Moving Missions*. http://movingmissions.org/wp-content/pdfs/mission-reinvention.pdf.
Grimes, Barbara F. *Ethnologue: Languages of the World*. Dallas, TX: SIL International, 2000.

Bibliography

Gupta, Paul Rajkumar. "Christian Missions and Economic Issues: Global, Institutional and Personal." Paper presented at the Overseas Ministries Study Center Conference on Missions and Money, New Haven, CT, 2005.

———. *Global Trends That Influence the Practice of Partnership with Indigenous Missions*, Paper presented at the COSIM Conference, Orlando, Florida, 2005.

———. "Institutionalization and Renewal of the Hindustan Bible Institute" PhD diss., Fuller Theological Seminary, 1992.

Hall, Edward T. *The Hidden Dimension*. New York: Anchor, 1990.

Hanks, Lucien Mason. "Merit and Power in the Thai Social Order." *American Anthropologist* 64 (1962) 1247–61.

Hatch, Elvin. *Respectable Lives: Social Standing in Rural New Zealand*. Berkeley, CA: University of California Press, 1992.

———. "Theories of Social Honor." *American Anthropologist* 91 (1989) 341–53.

Herzfeld, Michael. "'As in Your Own House': Hospitality, Ethnography, and the Stereotype of Mediterranean Society." In *Honor and Shame and the Unity of the Mediterranean*, edited by David D. Gilmore, 75–89. Washington, DC: American Anthropological Association, 1987.

———. "Honor and Shame: Problems in the Comparative Analysis of Moral Systems." *Man* 15 (1980) 339–51.

Hesselgrave, David J. *Communicating Christ Cross-Culturally*. Grand Rapids, MI: Zondervan, 1991.

Hiebert, Paul G. *Anthropological Insights for Missionaries*. Grand Rapids, MI: Baker, 1985.

Hill, Frances. *A Delusion of Satan: The Full Story of the Salem Witch Trials*. New York: De Capo, 1995.

Himmelman, Donald J. "Jesus' Eschatological Concern for Poor Folk: An Exegetical Study of Luke 6:20–21, 24–25." In *Vita Laudanda: Essays in Memory of Ulrich S. Leupold*, edited by Erich R. W. Schultz, 73–79. Waterloo, Ontario: Wilfred Laurier University Press, 1976.

Hoffer, Peter Charles. *The Salem Witchcraft Trials: A Legal History*. Lawrence, KS: University Press of Kansas, 1997.

Hofstede, Geert. *Culture's Consequences: Comparing Values, Behaviors, Institutions and Organizations Across Nations*. Thousand Oaks, CA: Sage, 2001.

———. "National Culture Dimensions." https://www.hofstede-insights.com/models/national-culture.

Hofstede, Geert, et al. *Cultures and Organizations*. 3rd ed. New York: McGraw-Hill, 2010.

Holmes, Henry, and Suchada Tangtongtavy. *Working with the Thais: A Guide to Managing in Thailand*. Bangkok: White Lotus, 1997.

Hu, Hsien Chin. "The Chinese Concepts of 'Face.'" *American Anthropologist* 46 (1944) 45–64.

Huffard, Evertt. "Thematic Dissonance in the Muslim-Christian Encounter: A Contextualized Theology of Honor." PhD diss., Fuller Theological Seminary, 1985.

Hughes, P. "Christianity and Buddhism in Thailand." *Journal of the Siam Society* 73 (1985) 23–41.

Human Rights Watch. "What Future? Street children in the Democratic Republic of Congo." *Human Rights Watch* 18.2A (2006). https://www.hrw.org/reports/2006/drc0406/drc0406web.pdf.

Hwang, Kwang-Kuo. "Face and Favor: The Chinese Power Game." *American Journal of Sociology* 92 (1987) 944–74.

Bibliography

"The Indian Partnership Act 1932." April 8, 1932. https://indiacode.nic.in/bitstream/123456789/4095/1/the_indian_partnership_act_1932.pdf.

Jackendoff, Ray. *Foundations of Language: Brain, Meaning, Grammar, Evolution*. Oxford: Oxford University Press, 2002.

Jacobs, N. *Absence of Absolute Standards: Clues to Thai Culture*. Bangkok: Kanok Bannasan, 1981.

———. *Modernization without Development: Thailand as an Asian Case Study*. New York: Praeger, 1971.

Jeong, Paul Yonggap. *Mission From a Position of Weakness*. New York: Peter Lang. 2012.

Johnson, Alan R. *Leadership in a Slum: A Bangkok Case Study*. Eugene, OR: Wipf and Stock, 2009.

Karen, Robert. "Shame." *Atlantic Monthly* (1992) 40–70.

Keating, Elizabeth. "Honor and Statification in Pohnpei, Micronesia." *American Ethnologist* 25 (1998) 399–411.

Klapp, Orin E. *Models of Social Order: An Introduction to Sociological Theory*. Palo Alto, CA: Mayfield, 1973.

Kluckhohn, Clyde. *Navaho Witchcraft*. Boston, MA: Beacon, 1944.

Koeshall, Anita L. "Toward a Theory of Dynamic Asymmetry and Redeemed Power: A Case Study of Reflexive Agents in German Pentecostal Churches." PhD diss., Fuller Theological Seminary, 2008.

Komin, Suntaree. "Culture and Work-Related Values in Thai Organizations." *International Journal of Psychology* 25 (1990) 681–704.

———. *Psychology of the Thai People: Values and Behavioral Patterns*. Bangkok: National Institute of Development Administration, 1991.

Kraus, C. Norman. *Jesus Christ Our Lord: Christology From a Disciple's Perspective*. Scottdale, PA: Herald, 1987.

Krauss, Michael. "The World's Languages in Crises." *Language* 68 (1992) 4–10.

Kressel, Gideon M., and Unni Wikan. "More on Honor and Shame." *Man* 23 (1988) 167–70.

La Fontaine, Jean. *The Devil's Children: From Spirit Possession to Witchcraft: New Allegations That Affect Children*. Surrey, UK: Ashgate, 2009.

Ladd, George Eldon. *The Gospel of the Kingdom: Scriptural Studies in the Kingdom of God*. Grand Rapids, MI: Eerdmans, 2011.

Lausanne Movement. "A Confession of Faith and a Call to Action." Lausanne Committee on World Evangelization, October 16–25, 2010, Cape Town, South Africa. https://www.lausanne.org/content/ctc/ctcommitment#capetown.

Leach, Edmund R. *Political Systems of Highland Burma: A Study of Kachin Social Structure*. Boston, MA: Beacon, 1954.

Lebra, Takie Sugiyama. "Shame and Guilt: A Psychocultural View of the Japanese Self." *Ethos* 11 (1983) 192–209.

———. "The Social Mechanism of Guilt and Shame: The Japanese Case." *Anthropological Quarterly* 44 (1971) 241–55.

Lederleitner, Mary. *Cross-Cultural Partnerships: Navigating the Complexities of Money and Mission*. Downers Grove, IL: InterVarsity, 2010.

Levasheff, Drake S. "Jesus of Nazareth, Paul of Tarsus, and the Early Christian Challenge to Traditional Honor and Shame Values." PhD diss., University of California, Los Angeles, 2013.

Levy, Robert I. "Introduction: Self and Emotion." *Ethos* 11 (1983) 128–34.

Bibliography

Lewis, M. Paul. *Ethnologue: Languages of the World.* Dallas, TX: SIL International, 2009.
Lewis, M. Paul, et al. *Ethnologue: Languages of the World.* Dallas, TX: SIL International, 2016.
Lewis, M. Paul, and Gary F. Simons. "Assessing Endangerment: Expanding Fishman's GIDS." *Revue Roumaine de Linguistique* 555 (2010) 103–20. http://www.lingv.ro/resources/scm_images/RRL-02-2010-Lewis.pdf.
Lewis, Richard D. *When Teams Collide: Managing the International Team Successfully.* London: Nicholas Brealey, 2012.
Lewis, Richard G. "How Cultures Work: A Roadmap for Intercultural Understanding in the Workplace." *Evangelical Missions Quarterly* 45 (2009) 38–45.
Lindisfarne, Nancy. "Gender, Shame, and Culture: An Anthropological Perspective." In *Shame: Interpersonal Behavior, Psychopathology, and Culture,* edited by Paul Gilbert and Bernice Andrews, 246–60. New York: Oxford University Press, 1998.
Linehard, Ruth. "A 'Good Conscience': Differences between Honor and Justice Orientation." *Missiology* 39 (2001) 131–41.
———. "Restoring Relationships: Theological Reflection on Shame and Honor among the Raba and Bana of Cameroon." PhD diss., Fuller Theological Seminary, 2000.
Lingenfelter, Sherwood G. *Agents of Transformation.* Grand Rapids, MI: Baker, 1996.
———. *Leading Cross-Culturally: Covenant Relationships for Effective Christian Leadership.* Grand Rapids, MI: Baker Academic, 2008.
———. *Ministering Cross-Culturally: An Incarnational Model for Personal Relationships.* Grand Rapids: Baker, 1986.
———. *Transforming Culture: A Challenge for Christian Mission.* Grand Rapids, MI: Baker, 1998.
Lingenfelter, Sherwood G., and Marvin Mayers. *Ministering Cross-Culturally: An Incarnational Model for Interpersonal Relationships.* Grand Rapids, MI: Baker Academic, 2003.
Livingood, Ellen. "Global Partnering Growing Pains." *Catalyst Interchange Postings Online* 4 (2012) 1–3. http://www.catalystservices.org/wp-content/uploads/2012/07/Ptshp-Chal.I.pdf.
Loewen, Jacob A. "The Social Context of Guilt and Forgiveness." *Practical Anthropology* 17 (1970) 80–96.
Lundy, David. "Moving Beyond Internationalizing the Mission Force." *International Journal of Frontier Missions* 16 (1999) 147–55. http://www.ijfm.org/PDFs_IJFM/16_3_PDFs/06%20Lundy.pdf.
Lynd, Helen Merrell. *On Shame and the Search for Identity.* New York: Science Editions, 1958.
Marden, John. "Self-Understanding of Thai: Targeting a Message So it Hits the Mark!" PhD diss., Presbyterian College and Theological Seminary, 1985.
Matsumoto, Yoshiko. "Reexamination of the Universality of Face: Politeness Phenomenon in Japanese." *Journal of Pragmatics* 12 (1988) 403–26.
Meyer, Birgit. *Translating the Devil: Religion and Modernity Among the Ewe in Ghana.* Edinburgh: Dinburgh University Press for the International African Institute, 1999.
Miller, William Ian. *Humiliation.* Ithaca, NY: Cornell University Press, 1993.
Milner, Murray, Jr. *Status and Sacredness: A General Theory of Status Relations and an Analysis of Indian Culture.* New York: Oxford University Press, 1994.
Mischke, Werner. *The Global Gospel: Achieving Missional Impact in Our Multicultural World.* Scottsdale, AZ: Mission One, 2015.

Bibliography

Modell, Judith. "The Wall of Shame: Ruth Benedict's Accomplishment in The Chrysanthemum and the Sword." *Dialectical Anthropology* 24 (1999) 193–215.
Molina, J. Aguilar. *The Invention of Child Witches in the Democratic Republic of Congo: Social Cleansing, Religious Commerce and the Difficulties of Being a Parent in an Urban Culture.* London: USAID, 2005.
Monsma, Karl. "The Meaning of Honor: A Case of Libel in Nineteenth-Century Rio Grande do Sul." Paper prepared for presentation at the XXI International Congress of the Latin American Studies Association, Chicago, September 24–26, 1998.
Mor Barak, Michelle E. *Managing Diversity: Toward a Globally Inclusive Workplace.* Thousand Oaks, CA: SAGE, 2011.
Moran, Robert T., et al. *Managing Cultural Differences.* Burlington, MA: Butterworth-Heinemann, 2010.
Moreau, A. Scott, et al. *Evangelical Dictionary of World Missions.* Grand Rapids, MI: Baker, 2000.
Muller, Roland. *Honor and Shame: Unlocking the Door.* Philadelphia: Xlibris, 2000.
Nathanson, Donald L. *Shame and Pride: Affect, Sex, and the Birth of the Self.* New York: Norton & Co., 1992.
Newbigin, Lesslie. *The Open Secret: An Introduction to the Theology of Mission.* Grand Rapids, MI: Eerdmans, 1995.
Neyrey, Jerome H. *The Social World of Luke-Acts: Models for Interpretation.* Peabody, MA: Hendrikson, 1991.
Nicoll, Peter. "Globalisation and International Mission." *Encounters Mission Ezine* 3 (2004). http://www.redcliffe.org/uploads/documents/intl_mission1_03.pdf.
Nida, Eugene. *Customs and Cultures.* Pasadena, CA: William Carey, 1975.
Niratpattanasai, Kriengsak. *Bridging the Gap.* Bangkok, Thailand: Asia, 2004.
———. "Overcoming Limited Belief." *Bangkok Post*, October 17, 2005.
Nurse, Derek. *Tense and Aspect in Bantu.* Oxford: Oxford University Press, 2008.
Nye, Robert A. *Masculinity and Male Codes of Honor in Modern France.* Berkeley, CA: University of California Press, 1998.
Onyinah, Opoku. "Contemporary 'Witchdemonology' in Africa." *International Review of Mission* 93 (2004) 330–45.
———. "Deliverance as a Way of Confronting Witchcraft in Modern Africa: Ghana as a Case History." *Cyberjournal for Pentecostal-Charismatic Research* 10 (2001). http://www.pctii.org/cyberj/cyberj10/onyinah.html.
Padilla, Catalina F. de, and Elsa Tamez. *La Relacion de Hombre-Mujer en Perspectiva Cristiana.* Buenos Aires: Ediciones Kairos, 2002.
Parsons, Talcott. *Sociological Theory and Modern Society.* New York: Free Press, 1967.
Pastner, Carroll McClure. "A Social Structural and Historical Analysis of Honor, Shame, and Purdah." *Anthropological Quarterly* 45 (1972) 248–61.
Patrick, Harold A., and Vincent Raj Kumar. "Managing Workplace Diversity: Issues and Challenges." *SAGE Open* 2.2 (2012) 1–15. http://sgo.sagepub.com/content/2/2/2158244012444615.full.pdf+html.
Pattison, Stephen. *Shame: Theory, Therapy, Theology.* Cambridge, UK: Cambridge University Press, 2000.
Peristiany, J. G. *Honor and Shame: The Values of Mediterranean Society.* London: Weidenfeld and Nicolson, 1965.
Persons, Larry Scott. "Face Dynamics, Social Power And Virtue Among Thai Leaders: A Cultural Analysis." PhD diss., Fuller Graduate School, 2008.

Bibliography

Phillips, Herbert P. *Thai Peasant Personality: The Patterning of Interpersonal Behavior in the Village of Bang Chan.* Berkeley, CA: University of California Press, 1965.
Piers, G., and M. B. Singer. *Shame and Guilt.* New York: Norton, 1953.
Pinker, Steven. *The Language Instinct: How the Mind Creates Language.* New York: Harper Perennial, 1994.
Pitt-Rivers, Julian A. *The Fate of Shechem (or the Politics of Sex): Essays in the Anthropology of the Mediterranean.* Cambridge, UK: Cambridge University Press, 1977.
Plumb-Takamoto, Susan. "Liminality and the North American Missionary Adjustment Process in Japan." PhD diss., Fuller Theological Seminary, 2003.
Prather, Craig M. "The Hispanic American "Man of the House": Analysis and Comparison of Cultural Machismo with the Servant Lifestyle of Biblical Manhood." PhD diss., Dallas Theological Seminary, 1999.
Priest, Robert J. "Witches and the Problem of Evil." *Books and Culture: A Christian Review* 15 (2009) 30–32.
Ranger, Terance. "Scotland Yard in the Bush: Medicine Murders, Child Witches and the Construction of the Occult: A Literature Review." *Africa* 77 (2007) 272–83.
Richards, E. Randolph, and Brandon J. O'Brien. *Misreading Scripture with Western Eyes: Removing Cultural Blinders to Better Understand the Bible.* Downers Grove, IL: InterVarsity, 2012.
Ridderbos, Herman. *The Coming of the Kingdom.* Edinburgh, UK: Christian World, 1979.
Roberts, Dana. "Missions in a Matrix of Movement." *Faith and Leadership*, September 27, 2010. https://www.faithandleadership.com/missions-matrix-movement.
Roembke, L. *Building Credible Multicultural Teams.* Pasadena, CA: William Carey, 2000.
Rosaldo, Michelle Z. "The Shame of Headhunters and the Autonomy of the Self." *Ethos* 11 (1983) 135–51.
Rosaldo, Renato. *Culture and Truth: The Remaking of Social Analysis.* Boston: Beacon, 1989.
Rynkiewich, Michael A. *Soul, Self, and Society: A Postmodern Anthropology for Mission in a Postcolonial World.* Eugene, OR: Cascade, 2011.
Samovar, Larry A., et al. *Communication Between Cultures.* Thousand Oaks, CA: Wadsworth, 2009.
Shin, H. S. *Principles of Church-Planting in Thai Theravada Buddhist Context.* Bangkok, Thailand: Kanok Bannasan, 1989.
Shuster, Marguerite. *Power, Pathology, Paradox: The Dynamics of Evil and Good.* Grand Rapids, MI: Zondervan, 1987.
Shweder, Richard. *Why Do Men Barbecue?: Recipes for Cultural Psychology.* Boston: Harvard University Press, 2003.
Siegel, Lee. *Net of Magic: Wonders and Deceptions in India.* Chicago: University of Chicago Press, 1991.
Simons, Gary F. "Language Development Versus Language Endangerment: Assessing the Situation Worldwide." Paper presented at the IAS and GILLBT Conference on Language and Culture in National Development, University of Ghana, Legon, April 12–13, 2012. https://scholars.sil.org/sites/scholars/files/gary_f_simons/presentation/ghana_2012.pdf.
Smith, Donald. *Creating Understanding: A Handbook for Christian Communication Across Cultural Landscapes.* Grand Rapids, MI: Zondervan, 1992.
Snit, Smuckarn. "Ruang Na Khong Khon Thai: Wikhro Tam Naokwamkit Tang Manusyawithayapasasat (Concerning the 'Face' of Thai People: Analysis According

Bibliography

to the Anthropological Linguistics Approach)." *Thai Journal of Development Administration* 15 (1975) 492–505.

Stevens, Evelyn P., and Ann Pescatello. *Marianismo: The Other Face of Machismo in Latin America*. Pittsburgh: University of Pittsburgh Press, 1973.

Stewart, Charles. "Honor and Shame." In *International Encyclopedia of the Social and Behavioral Sciences*, edited by James D. Wright, 11:181–84. Amsterdam: Elsevier, 2015.

Stewart, Frank H. *Honor*. Chicago: University of Chicago Press, 1994.

Strecker, Ivo. "Do the Hamar Have a Concept of Honor?" South Omo Research Center. https://web.archive.org/web/20110725090010/http://www.uni-mainz.de/Organisationen/SORC/fileadmin/texts/Do%20the%20Hamar%20have%20a%20Concept%20of%20Honor.pdf.

Sundquist, Scott, et al., eds. *A Dictionary of Asian Christianity*. Grand Rapids, MI: Eerdmans, 2001.

———. *Psychology of the Thai People: Values and Behavioral Patterns*. Bangkok: National Institute of Development Administration, Research Center, 1990.

Tamez, Elsa. *Against Machismo*. Oak Park, IL: Meyer Stone, 1987.

Tannehill, Robert C. *The Narrative Unity of Luke-Acts: A Literary Interpretation*. Vol. 1. Philadelphia: Fortress, 1994.

Taylor, Charles. *Sources of the Self: The Making of the Modern Identity*. Cambridge, MA: Harvard University Press, 1989.

Taylor, Gabriele. *Pride, Shame, and Guilt: Emotions of Self-Assessment*. Oxford: Clarendon, 1985.

Taylor, S. "Gaps in Beliefs of Thai Christians." *Evangelical Missions Quarterly* 17 (2001) 72–81.

———. *Patron Client Relationships and the Challenge for the Thai Church*. Bangkok, Thailand: Discipleship Training Center, 1997.

Tennent, Timothy C. *Theology in the Context of World Christianity: How the Global Church Is Influencing the Way We Think About and Discuss Theology*. Grand Rapids, MI: Zondervan, 2009.

Terweil, B. J. "Formal Structure and Informal Rules: An Historical Perspective on Hierarchy, Bondage and the Patron-Client Relationship." *Strategies and Structures in Thai Society*. Amsterdam: University of Amsterdam, 1984.

———. *A Window on Thai History*. Bangkok: Duang Kamol, 1989.

Thiselton, Anthony C. *The First Epistle to the Corinthians: A Commentary on the Greek Text*. New International Greek Testament Commentary. Grand Rapids, MI: Eerdmans, 2000.

Thomas, Keith. *Religion and the Decline of Magic*. New York: Scribner's Sons, 1971.

Thompson, M., et al. *Culture Theory*. Boulder, CO: Westview, 1990.

Ting-Toomey, Stella, ed. *The Challenge of Facework: Cross-Cultural and Interpersonal Issues*. New York: State University of New York Press, 1994.

Torres, J. B., et al. "The Myth of Sameness among Latino Men and Their Machismo." *American Journal Orthopsychiatry* 72 (2002) 163–181.

Trebesch, Shelley G. *Isolation: A Place of Transformation in the Life of a Leader*. Altadena, CA: Barnabas, 1997.

Turner, V. W. *The Ritual Process: Structure and Anti-Structure*. Ithaca, NY: Cornell University Press, 1969.

Bibliography

Ukosakul, Margaret. "Conceptual Metaphors Motivating the Use of Thai 'Face.'" MA thesis, Payap University, 1999.
Van Engen, Charles. "Specialization/Integration in Mission Education." *Missiological Education for the Twenty-First Century*. Maryknoll, NY: Orbis, 1996.
Volf, Miroslav. *Exclusion and Embrace: A Theological Exploration of Identity, Otherness, and Reconciliation*. Nashville, TN Abingdon, 1996.
———. "Living with the Other." *Journal of Ecumenical Studies* 39 (2002) 8–25.
Watters, John R. "Syntax." In *African Languages: An Introduction*, edited by Bernd Heine and Derek Nurse, 194–230. Cambridge, UK: Cambridge University Press, 2000.
Weber, Max. *Basic Concepts in Sociology*. Translated by H. P. Secher. New York: Carol, 1993.
———. *Selections in Translation*. edited by W. G. Runciman. Translated by E. Matthews. Cambridge, UK: Cambridge University Press, 1978.
Whalen, D. H., and Gary F. Simons. "Endangered Language Families." *Language* 88 (2012) 155–73.
Whiteman, Darrell. "Anthropology and Mission: The Incarnational Connection (Part I)." *International Journal of Frontier Missions* 20.4 (2003) 35–44. http://www.ijfm.org/PDFs_IJFM/21_1_PDFs/35_44_Whiteman2.pdf.
———. "Anthropology and Mission: The Incarnational Connection (Part II)." *International Journal of Frontier Mission* 21.2 (2004) 79–88. http://www.ijfm.org/PDFs_IJFM/21_2_PDFs/79_Whiteman.pdf.
Wickeri, Philip L. *Partnership, Solidarity, and Friendship: Transforming Structures in Mission*. Louisville: Worldwide Ministries, 2003. http://www.pcusa.org/media/uploads/worldmission/pdfs/transforming_structures_in_mission_-_wickeri.pdf.
Wikkan, Unni. "Shame and Honor: A Contestable Pair." *Man* 19 (1984) 635–52.
Wildavsky, A. *The Nursing Father: Moses as a Political Leader*. Tuscaloosa, AL: University of Alabama Press, 1984.
Wilson, Steven R., and Adrianne W. Kunkel. "Identity Implications of Influence Goals: Similarities in Perceived Face Threats and Facework Across Sex and Close Relationships." *Journal of Language and Social Psychology* 19 (2000) 195–221.
Wolf, Eric J. *Envisioning Power: Ideologies of Dominance in Crisis*. Berkeley, CA: University of California Press, 1999.
Wu, Jackson. *Saving God's Face: A Chinese Contextualization of Salvation Through Honor and Shame*. Pasadena, CA: William Carey, 2013.
Wyatt, D. K. *Thailand: A Short History*. London: Yale University Press, 1984.
Wyatt-Brown, Bertram. "Honor's History across the Academy." *Historically Speaking: The Bulletin of the Historical Society* 3 (2002) 13–15.
Yau-Fai Ho, David. "On the Concept of Face." *American Journal of Sociology* 81 (1976) 867–84.
Zehner, Edwin. "Social Honor and Systems of Meaning: A Comment Inspired by Hatch." *American Anthropologist* 92 (1990) 1020–21.
Zolling, Peter. *Deutsche Geschichte von 1871 bis zur Gegenwart: Wie Deutschland wurde, was es ist*. München: Carl Hanser Verlag, 2005.

After a distinguished career at SUNY Brockport, Biola University, and Fuller Theological Seminary, Sherwood Lingenfelter recently retired from full-time teaching and administrative leadership. On the occasion of his retirement and as a celebration of the far-reaching impact he has had on the missiological community, former students and esteemed colleagues have submitted these chapters as a way of highlighting Sherwood's immense impact. His global influence is a result of a passionate committed to excellent mentoring, teaching, and the very highest quality of equipping for missionaries and mission organizations. Those who know Sherwood Lingenfelter understand well the carefully selected title of this collection of essays. His deepest passion is to serve and honor Christ. Indeed, his distinguished career of missiological excellence flows from a life fully devoted to Christ. It is with a spirit of gratitude that his students, friends, and colleagues offer the essays in this Festschrift. We celebrate the teaching, writing, and consulting ministry of a leading western missiological voice, Sherwood G. Lingenfelter.

About the Editor: Christopher L. Flanders is Associate Professor of Missions at Abilene Christian University. He formerly served as a missionary in Thailand.

Contributors: Lorraine Dierck, Donna R. Downes, Paul R. Gupta, Paul Yonggap Jeong, Anita Koeshall, C. Douglas McConnell, Larry S. Persons, Robert J. Priest, Wilmer Villacorta, John R. Watters, and Alan Weaver.

www.ingramcontent.com/pod-product-compliance
Lightning Source LLC
Chambersburg PA
CBHW051744230426
43670CB00012B/2148